Test-Item File to Accompany
Introduction to Sociology
Fourth Edition

Test-Item File to Accompany
Introduction to Sociology
Fourth Edition

Stu Shafer
Johnson County Community College

W. W. NORTON & COMPANY • NEW YORK • LONDON

Composition and layout by Roberta Flechner Graphics

ISBN 0-393-97843-5 (pbk.)

W. W. Norton & Company, Inc., 500 Fifth Avenue, New York, NY 10110
www.wwnorton.com

W. W. Norton & Company Ltd., Castle House, 75/76 Wells Street, London W1T 3QT

1 2 3 4 5 6 7 8 9 0

CONTENTS

Test-Item File to Accompany

Introduction to Sociology

Fourth Edition

CHAPTER 1

What Is Sociology?

Multiple-Choice Questions

d (page 1)
1. Sociology is the scientific study of
   a. human social life.
   b. groups.
   c. societies.
   d. All of the above
   e. None of the above

c (page 2)
2. From a sociological perspective, the love you feel for a romantic partner is
   a. natural.
   b. universal.
   c. a product of particular historical and cultural circumstances.
   d. All of the above
   e. None of the above

c (pages 5–6)
3. Who came up with the idea of a "sociological imagination"?
   a. Anthony Giddens
   b. Karl Marx
   c. Wright Mills
   d. Max Weber
   e. Emile Durkheim

b (page 6)
4. What is it called when we "think ourselves away" from the familiar routine in order to see things in a different, more sociological perspective?
   a. romanticism
   b. sociological imagination
   c. multiple personality disorder
   d. globalization
   e. unintended consequences

1

c (page 6)

5. The significance of a sociological imagination is that
   a. sociology should be considered a philosophy rather than a science.
   b. sociologists are primarily interested in predicting the future.
   c. sociology attempts to understand personal events in social contexts.
   d. sociology is not concerned with empirical verification of theories.
   e. sociologists imagine that studying sociology will lead to revolutions.

a (pages 6–7)

6. According to the sociological perspective, people's behavior
   a. is influenced by the social context.
   b. is entirely determined by the social context.
   c. has nothing to do with social context.
   d. is mostly a result of their genes.
   e. is mostly a result of their personality.

d (page 7)

7. What is the meaning of "social structure"?
   a. any building constructed by more than one person
   b. random events or actions
   c. the mental state or personality of an individual
   d. a regularity or pattern in the way people behave and in their relationships to one another
   e. a major feature of the natural landscape

b (page 7)

8. People who are shaped by the social structure are constantly reconstructing those same social structures. What word does the text use to refer to this process?
   a. sociological imagination
   b. structuration
   c. ·socialism
   d. globalization
   e. None of the above; the text does not use such a concept.

e (page 10)

9. Our lives today are increasingly interdependent with other people, even those who are thousands of miles away. This rapid process of social change creating connections between the local and the global is known as
    a. socialization.
    b. creeping communism.
    c. functionalism.
    d. localization.
    e. globalization.

b (page 11)

10. _____ shows *how* things occur; _____ considers *why* things happen.
    a. Theory; factual research
    b. Factual research; theory
    c. Sociology; psychology
    d. Psychology; sociology
    e. Astronomy; astrology

a (page 11)

11. Which of the following uses interpretation to explain a wide range of observed facts and situations?
    a. theory
    b. factual research
    c. globalization
    d. romantic love
    e. social structure

d (page 12)

12. Which of the following was an important factor behind the emergence of sociological thinking?
    a. new political forms and ideas, such as those expressed in the French Revolution
    b. new economic forms created in the Industrial Revolution
    c. new ways of understanding the world in scientific rather than religious terms
    d. All of the above
    e. None of the above

c (pages 12–13)

13. When and where did the perspective calling itself sociology emerge?
    a. 500 years B.C.E., China
    b. first century, Rome
    c. early 1800s, Europe
    d. early 1900s, United States
    e. mid 1900s, Europe

a (page 12)   14. Which sociological theorist invented the word "sociology"?
                     a. Auguste Comte
                     b. Emile Durkheim
                     c. Karl Marx
                     d. Max Weber
                     e. Anthony Giddens

c (page 12)   15. What should the knowledge of society be based on,
                     according to Auguste Comte?
                     a. religion
                     b. physics
                     c. scientific evidence
                     d. miracles
                     e. tradition

a (page 13)   16. According to Durkheim, society is
                     a. greater than the sum of its parts.
                     b. equal to the sum of its parts.
                     c. less than the sum of its parts.
                     d. indivisible into individual parts.
                     e. inconceivable as a whole.

c (page 13)   17. What did Émile Durkheim call aspects of social life that
                     influence and shape our individual actions?
                     a. social structure
                     b. social transformation
                     c. social facts
                     d. unintended consequences
                     e. romantic love

b (page 13)   18. In order for a complex society to function properly,
                     according to Émile Durkheim, all its parts must work
                     together as an integrated whole. He referred to this social
                     cohesion as
                     a. mechanical solidarity.
                     b. organic solidarity.
                     c. solidarity integration.
                     d. solidarity cohesion.
                     e. solidarity forever.

d (page 13)   19. Émile Durkheim analyzed the social changes transforming
                     society in his lifetime in terms of
                     a. "social physics".
                     b. the materialist conception of history.
                     c. the rationalization of social and economic life.
                     d. the division of labor.
                     e. symbolic interactionism.

c (page 14)

20. Which early theorist saw class conflict as the main source of social change?
    a. Auguste Comte
    b. Émile Durkheim
    c. Karl Marx
    d. Max Weber
    e. Anthony Giddens

c (page 14)

21. According to Karl Marx, the modern era is shaped primarily by
    a. anomie.
    b. bureaucracy.
    c. capitalism.
    d. division of labor.
    e. enemies of the state.

d (page 14)

22. Karl Marx's ideas influenced
    a. Soviet Communism.
    b. governments over more than a third of the world's population until recently.
    c. many sociologists.
    d. All of the above
    e. None of the above

d (pages 14–15)

23. Which of the following was a focus of Max Weber's research?
    a. the distinctiveness of Western society as contrasted with other civilizations
    b. the influence of cultural ideas and values on social change and individual behavior
    c. bureaucracy
    d. All of the above
    e. None of the above

e (page 16)

24. Who had the greatest influence on the theoretical approach known as symbolic interactionism?
    a. Auguste Comte
    b. Émile Durkheim
    c. Karl Marx
    d. Max Weber
    e. George Herbert Mead

c (page 14) 25. What played the fundamental role in developing the capitalistic outlook, according to Max Weber?
    a. organic solidarity
    b. capitalism
    c. religious values
    d. symbolic interaction
    e. feminism

d (page 18) 26. In the classical period of sociology, _____ were rarely allowed to hold academic positions or do sociological research, so their contributions have been neglected.
    a. men
    b. French men
    c. Germans
    d. women and minorities
    e. Europeans

c (page 18) 27. Who was "the first woman sociologist"?
    a. Émile Durkheim
    b. Emily Dickinson
    c. Harriet Martineau
    d. W. E. B. Du Bois
    e. Maxine Weber

c (page 18) 28. Who wrote the following statement? "The nursery, the boudoir, and the kitchen are all excellent schools in which to learn the morals and manners of a people."
    a. Émile Durkheim
    b. Emily Dickinson
    c. Harriet Martineau
    d. W. E. B. Du Bois
    e. Maxine Weber

d (pages 18–19) 29. W. E. B. Du Bois used the concept of _____ to refer to the particular experience of African Americans as they were forced to see themselves through the eyes of others.
    a. organic solidarity
    b. rationalization
    c. dialectical materialism
    d. double consciousness
    e. None of the above

d (page 19)

30. Who said about American society, "the problem of the twentieth century is the problem of the color line"?
   a. Émile Durkheim
   b. George Herbert Mead
   c. Harriet Martineau
   d. W. E. B. Du Bois
   e. C. Wright Mills

a (page 20)

31. Gender, class, and race are concepts at the heart of _____ sociology.
   a. feminist
   b. functionalist
   c. symbolic interactionist
   d. All of the above
   e. None of the above

b (page 13)

32. Which sociologist showed that social factors exert a fundamental influence on suicidal behavior?
   a. Auguste Comte
   b. Émile Durkheim
   c. Karl Marx
   d. Max Weber
   e. Anthony Giddens

c (page 17)

33. What is involved in nearly all social interactions, according to symbolic interactionists?
   a. conflict
   b. an exchange of functions
   c. an exchange of symbols
   d. a feeling of despair or aimlessness
   e. All of the above

c (page 17)

34. Which theoretical approach uses the analogy of the human body in assessing the role of each part of society in the continuation of society as a whole?
   a. Marxism
   b. symbolic interactionism
   c. functionalism
   d. feminism
   e. All of the above

d (page 17)   35. Who was particularly influential in the development of
                   functionalism?
                   a. Karl Marx
                   b. Max Weber
                   c. George Herbert Mead
                   d. Robert K. Merton
                   e. W. E. B. Du Bois

b (page 20)   36. How does Marxism differ from other theoretical traditions
                   (functionalism and symbolic interactionism) in sociology?
                   a. Marxism is not concerned with political reform.
                   b. Marxists put more emphasis on class conflict, power,
                       and ideology.
                   c. Marxism is currently the most influential of the three.
                   d. All of the above
                   e. None of the above

a (page 20)   37. If a person or group is able to make their own concerns or
                   interests count, even if others resist, that individual or
                   group has
                   a. power.
                   b. ideology.
                   c. symbol.
                   d. relative deprivation.
                   e. All of the above

a (page 20)   38. What do Marxism and feminism have in common?
                   a. Both focus on inequalities and conflict as central
                       features of modern societies.
                   b. Neither sees advocating social change as an
                       appropriate activity for sociologists.
                   c. Both reject the idea that subordinate groups are worthy
                       of study.
                   d. All of the above
                   e. None of the above

a (page 17)   39. Which theoretical perspective emphasizes the significance
                   of moral consensus in social life?
                   a. functionalism
                   b. Marxism
                   c. symbolic interactionism
                   d. rational choice theory
                   e. feminism

c (page 21)   40. Behavior that is oriented toward self-interest is often called
                       a. affective action.
                       b. effective action.
                       c. instrumental or rational action.
                       d. habit.
                       e. higher values.

e (pages 21–22)   41. According to postmodernist theory,
                       a. history is leading us inevitably toward socialism.
                       b. society is becoming increasingly homogenized.
                       c. the nation-state is growing stronger.
                       d. All of the above
                       e. None of the above

a (page 22)   42. What is the main source of meaning in the postmodern
                       world, according to Baudrillard?
                       a. images in the media
                       b. religion
                       c. habit
                       d. class consciousness
                       e. self-interest

e (page 21)   43. Which theoretical perspective holds that the grand
                       narratives that gave meaning to history in the past no
                       longer make any sense?
                       a. Functionalism
                       b. Marxism
                       c. Weberianism
                       d. symbolic interactionism
                       e. postmodernism

c (page 11)   44. Which of the following are more narrowly focused efforts
                       to explain particular social conditions or types of event?
                       a. symbols
                       b. concepts
                       c. theories
                       d. theoretical approaches
                       e. None of the above

a (page 23)

45. The study of everyday life and face-to-face interaction is called
    a. microsociology.
    b. macrosociology.
    c. biosociology.
    d. sychosociology.
    e. None of the above

b (page 23)

46. Analysis of large-scale systems and long-term processes is known as
    a. microsociology.
    b. macrosociology.
    c. biosociology.
    d. psychosociology.
    e. None of the above

c (page 24)

47. Sociology uses systematic methods of empirical investigation, the analysis of data, theoretical thinking, and the logical assessment of arguments to develop a body of knowledge. Therefore, it is a(n)
    a. ideology.
    b. religion.
    c. science.
    d. All of the above
    e. None of the above

d (page 25)

48. Which of the following is a practical benefit of the study of sociology?
    a. increased awareness and understanding of cultural differences
    b. ability to assess the effects, including unintended consequences, of public policies
    c. increased self-understanding
    d. All of the above
    e. None of the above

True/False Questions

F (page 2)

1. It is natural to associate romantic love with marriage, as all known human societies do.

T (page 6)

2. With a sociological imagination, one sees personal troubles, such as divorce, in terms of larger public issues.

T (page 7)   3. What we do as individuals structures the social world and
                       is simultaneously structured *by* the social world around us.

F (pages 10–11)   4. People today live pretty much the same way they have for
                       the last 10,000 years: in large, industrialized towns and
                       cities.

F (page 11)   5. Fortunately, sociology has avoided the kinds of quarrels
                       and debates that characterize other sciences.

F (page 14)   6. Karl Marx urged sociologists to "study social facts as
                       things."

F (page 17)   7. Manifest functions are results of an activity which
                       participants are not aware of and did not intend.

T (page 20)   8. Feminism is a major, influential movement within
                       sociology today.

F (page 23)   9. Theoretical debate in sociology is a sign of its weakness as
                       a science.

T (page 23)   10. Microsociology and macrosociology depend on one
                       another.

Essay Questions

1. Use your sociological imagination to draw lessons from the attacks on the World
   Trade Center and the war on terrorism that followed. Be sure to discuss the
   structure of Osama bin Laden's organization as well as the *large-scale global
   processes* that underlay the events.

2. Can one become a sociologist by simply acquiring a set of facts and knowledge?
   What else is required for a sociological perspective? Explain, and show the
   relationship between facts and this other component.

3. Chapter One used the example of coffee to explain how one can apply a
   sociological perspective to an apparently mundane aspect of daily life. Use a
   similar approach to discuss what a Sociology of Shoes might reveal.

4. Discuss the process of structuration. How are the actions of individual human
   beings shaped by the social structure, while simultaneously helping to give
   structure to that society?

5. Why is a global perspective an essential component of sociology at this point in time? What is the relationship between the local and the global? What is the name of this process? How does it affect you personally?

6. What is a theory? Why are theories needed in sociology? What is the relationship between theories and facts?

7. What is a theoretical approach? What is the role of theoretical approaches in the development of sociological knowledge?

8. Compare the theoretical approaches of Marx, Durkheim, and Weber by contrasting their respective interpretations of modern development.

9. Discuss at least four ways sociology can make a difference in your world.

CHAPTER 2
Asking and Answering Sociological Questions

Multiple-Choice Questions

d (page 31)

1. Good sociological work involves
   a. precise questions.
   b. factual evidence.
   c. conclusions based on factual evidence.
   d. All of the above
   e. None of the above

a (page 30)

2. When Laud Humphreys studied the hidden world of the "tearoom trade," his research
   a. included participant observation and survey methods.
   b. allowed him to separate himself from the activities of his subjects so that he could remain completely objective.
   c. revealed nothing people didn't already know about through their own casual observations.
   d. All of the above
   e. None of the above

b (page 31)

3. Research questions which relate and contrast one social context with others are _____ questions.
   a. factual or empirical
   b. comparative
   c. theoretical
   d. developmental
   e. None of the above

b (page 31)

4. When sociologists conduct research they should
   a. be completely dispassionate about the subject they are studying.
   b. use theory to guide their research.
   c. avoid the application of theoretical perspectives in analyzing their results.
   d. All of the above
   e. None of the above

a (page 31)

5. "How many households in the United States are formed by two or more unmarried adults living together?" _____ questions like this might lead to important findings in a census report.
   a. Empirical
   b. Comparative
   c. Developmental
   d. Theoretical
   e. None of the above. This is not a sociological research question.

b (page 31)

6. A researcher contrasts the frequency of unmarried couple households in the past three decennial censuses and presents an explanation of the changes. Which type of research question is this?
   a. factual
   b. comparative
   c. developmental
   d. theoretical
   e. speculative

a (page 31)

7. _____ questions concern *how* things occur and involve the collection of facts; _____ questions concern *why* they occur, and involve the interpretation of facts.
   a. Empirical; theoretical
   b. Empirical; comparative
   c. Theoretical; empirical
   d. Theoretical; comparative
   e. Comparative; developmental

d (page 33)

8. All research begins with
   a. a hypothesis.
   b. conclusions.
   c. the research design.
   d. a research problem.
   e. review of existing evidence.

d (page 33)

9. Good, puzzle-solving research
   a. seeks to fill a gap in our understanding.
   b. seeks to go beyond mere descriptions of what is happening.
   c. seeks to contribute to our understanding of *why* things happen the way they do.
   d. All of the above
   e. None of the above

a (page 33)

10. Which of these is the *prerequisite* to good sociological research?
   a. good sociological questions
   b. good sociological answers
   c. an advanced degree from a prestigious program
   d. All of the above
   e. None of the above

b (page 33)

11. Which step follows the selection of a research problem?
   a. statement of hypothesis
   b. review of existing evidence
   c. interpretation of results
   d. developing an appropriate research design
   e. reporting the findings

c (page 33)

12. Which step in the research process may involve formulation of a definite hypothesis?
   a. defining the research problem
   b. reviewing the available evidence
   c. making the problem precise
   d. developing an appropriate research design
   e. reporting the findings

e (page 34)

13. What is the final step in a research project?
   a. statement of hypothesis
   b. review of existing evidence
   c. interpretation of results
   d. developing an appropriate research design
   e. reporting the findings

b (page 35)

14. If one event or situation produces another, the two are said to have a
   a. hypothesis.
   b. causal relationship.
   c. methodology.
   d. symbolic interaction.
   e. theoretical approach.

c (page 35)

15. A _____ is any dimension along which individuals or groups vary.
   a. causation
   b. correlation
   c. variable
   d. control
   e. parallel universe

b (page 35)

16. A regular relationship between variables is known as a
    a. causation.
    b. correlation.
    c. variable.
    d. control.
    e. parallel universe.

c (page 36)

17. A(n) _____ is one that produces an effect on another variable.
    a. correlation
    b. dependent variable
    c. independent variable
    d. concept
    e. theory

b (page 36)

18. A(n) _____ is affected by a(n) _____.
    a. causation; correlation
    b. dependent variable; independent variable
    c. independent variable; dependent variable
    d. hypothesis; control
    e. cause; effect

c (page 36)

19. "The better the grades an individual gets in school, the better paying job he is likely to get." Grades are the _____ and occupational income is the _____.
    a. causation; correlation
    b. dependent variable; independent variable
    c. independent variable; dependent variable
    d. hypothesis; control
    e. effect; cause

d (page 36)

20. Variables that are held constant in order to test the effects of other variables are known as
    a. correlations.
    b. dependent variables.
    c. independent variables.
    d. controls.
    e. testers.

a (page 37)

21. Which research method would give a rich, detailed, inside view of a particular group, setting, or subculture?
    a. ethnography
    b. survey
    c. life history
    d. experiment
    e. comparative historical analysis

d (page 38)

22. Which of the following is an advantage of fieldwork as a research method?
    a. It provides richer information about social situations than other methods.
    b. It allows us to see a situation from the inside of a particular group.
    c. It gives the researcher greater flexibility to adjust to different situations.
    d. All of the above
    e. None of the above

b (page 38)

23. What is one of the most difficult parts of fieldwork?
    a. selecting a random sample
    b. gaining the trust of the subjects of the study
    c. finding sufficient archival sources
    d. writing the standardized questionnaire
    e. There are no difficulties in fieldwork.

b (page 38)

24. Which research method would be best to use if one wants a large, representative sample of people's attitudes toward an issue?
    a. ethnography
    b. survey
    c. life history
    d. experiment
    e. comparative historical analysis

c (page 38)

25. Which type of questionnaire provides respondents with a set of questions to which only a fixed-choice or limited set of responses is allowed?
    a. fieldwork
    b. experiment
    c. standardized
    d. open-ended
    e. despondent

d (page 38)

26. Which type of questionnaire allows respondents to give their own answers to questions, thus providing more detail and allowing researchers to ask follow-up questions?
    a. historical analysis
    b. experiment
    c. standardized
    d. open-ended
    e. despondent

b (page 39)

27. What is a pilot study?
    a. a study of people who fly airplanes
    b. a trial run of a survey to find potential problems with the questionnaire
    c. the final version of a questionnaire
    d. a study conducted by licensed researchers
    e. None of the above

c (page 39)

28. A _____ is a smaller proportion of a larger group selected for study.
    a. population
    b. control group
    c. sample
    d. standardized group
    e. None of the above

a (page 39)

29. In order for a sample to accurately reflect the characteristics of the study population it must be
    a. representative.
    b. democratic.
    c. public.
    d. open-ended.
    e. standardized.

e (page 39)

30. A sample is chosen in such a way that every member of the population has an equal chance of being selected. This process is called
    a. standardized sampling.
    b. open-ended sampling.
    c. field sampling.
    d. controlled sampling.
    e. random sampling.

a (page 40)

31. Which of the following is an advantage of survey research?
    a. Results can be easily quantified and analyzed.
    b. It allows us to see a situation from the inside of a particular group.
    c. It provides richer detail about a population than other methods.
    d. All of the above
    e. None of the above

b (page 40)   32. What research method tests hypotheses under highly
                       controlled conditions?
                       a. fieldwork
                       b. experiment
                       c. survey
                       d. historical analysis
                       e. life history

c (page 41)   33. Studying a period of the recent past by interviewing people
                       who witnessed events makes use of
                       a. experiment.
                       b. random sampling.
                       c. oral history.
                       d. All of the above
                       e. None of the above

e (page 42)   34. A sociologist who makes use of sources such as documents
                       and records kept in special collections called archives is
                       conducting
                       a. an experiment.
                       b. random sampling.
                       c. oral history.
                       d. fieldwork.
                       e. historical analysis.

a (page 41)   35. Sociologists engage in historical analysis because
                       a. a time perspective is frequently needed to make sense
                           of a research problem.
                       b. sociology is ill equipped to study the modern world.
                       c. survey research and fieldwork are inadequate research
                           methods.
                       d. a good sociologist must also be a good historian.
                       e. societies were more complex in the nineteenth century.

d (page 43)   36. The use of two or more methods of research to check up on
                       the others is called
                       a. scientology.
                       b. standard deviation.
                       c. correlation coefficient.
                       d. triangulation.
                       e. open-ended surveying.

d (page 46)   37. The results of sociological research often become widely
                       known in society, thus affecting the social life sociologists
                       study. This interaction between sociological research and
                       human behavior is known as a _____ relation.
                       a. human
                       b. control
                       c. standardized
                       d. reflexive
                       e. refractive

c (page 47)   38. In sociological research, various ways of calculating
                       averages are called
                       a. correlations.
                       b. controls.
                       c. measures of central tendency.
                       d. measures of mediocrity.
                       e. standard deviations.

a (page 47)   39. The measure of how much one variable relates to another
                       in a consistent way is the
                       a. correlation coefficient.
                       b. measure of central tendency.
                       c. standard deviation.
                       d. standard of conformity.
                       e. mode.

a (page 47)   40. If you add all the numbers in a series of data, then divide
                       by the number of cases, you have calculated the
                       a. mean.
                       b. median.
                       c. mode.
                       d. standard deviation.
                       e. correlation coefficient.

b (page 47)   41. Take the following series of numbers: 0, 1, 3, 5, 6. What is
                       the mean?
                       a. 1
                       b. 3
                       c. 5
                       d. 6
                       e. 15

c (page 47)

42. What is the most frequent figure in a series of numbers called?
    a. mean
    b. median
    c. mode
    d. standard deviation
    e. correlation coefficient

a (page 47)

43. In the following series of numbers, what is the mode?
    1, 1, 2, 6
    a. 1
    b. 2
    c. 6
    d. 10
    e. 1.5

a (page 47)

44. In the following series of numbers, what is the median?
    1, 3, 6
    a. 3
    b. 4
    c. 5
    d. 6
    e. 10

b (page 47)

45. What do statisticians call the middle number in a series?
    a. mean
    b. median
    c. mode
    d. standard deviation
    e. correlation coefficient

d (page 47)

46. What calculation gives a researcher a good idea of the range of a series of figures?
    a. mean
    b. median
    c. mode
    d. standard deviation
    e. correlation coefficient

b (page 47)

47. If two variables were completely correlated, their correlation coefficient would be
    a. 0.
    b. 1.
    c. 10.
    d. 100.
    e. nonexistent.

c (page 48)

48. What should be your first step when reading a table?
    a. Skip it. Tables are rarely important in sociology.
    b. Read the footnotes; they contain the most important information.
    c. Read the full title. It is the researcher's attempt to describe the data in the table.
    d. Draw your own pre-conclusions. Then you can judge whether the data are right.
    e. Always read from right to left; the idea of tables originated in the Middle East.

a (page 47)

49. Which of the following statistical terms refers to the "average"?
    a. mean
    b. mode
    c. median
    d. standard deviation
    e. middle

True/False Questions

T (page 31)

1. The results of sociological research often challenge our commonsense beliefs.

F (page 34)

2. All sociological research projects must follow the same steps precisely.

F (page 35)

3. If you observe a correlation you have observed causation.

T (page 36)

4. Sociologists can never be sure they have covered all possible causes in a correlation.

T (page 38)

5. A disadvantage of participant observation is that only small groups or communities can be studied this way.

F (page 39)

6. The only valid way to study a large population is to include every member of the population in the study group.

T (page 41)

7. Life histories often use sources like newspapers and contemporary descriptions to supplement the subject's account.

T (page 46)   8. The results of sociological research often become so widely known that people consider that knowledge to be "common sense."

F (page 47)   9. There is only one way to calculate an average in statistics—divide the total of a series of numbers by the number of cases.

Essay Questions

1. Discuss the types of questions a sociologist might ask when conducting research that is:
   a. factual
   b. comparative
   c. developmental
   d. theoretical
   Give an example of each.

2. What research methods did Humphreys employ when studying the "tearoom trade"? Why was this an appropriate research strategy? What advantages were gained in this approach? What were the disadvantages?

3. List the steps in the scientific research process and discuss what happens in each step.

4. What does it mean to say that scientific knowledge is a cumulative process? How does this accumulation take place? Is there just an addition of new knowledge on top of old knowledge, or does refinement also take place? Explain.

5. What is a causal relationship? What is a correlation? What, if any, is the difference between causation and correlation?

6. Which method or methods would most likely provide evidence of causation? Why?

7. Which method or methods would most likely show evidence of correlation between variables? Would that be conclusive evidence of causation? Explain.

8. A sociologist wishes to gain insight into the street vendor scene in a major American city. What research method would probably be best to use in such a study? Why?

9. Would it ever be desirable to use more than one method in a study? Explain.

10. Is it ever appropriate for a sociologist to conduct research without the knowledge of the subjects being studied? Explain.

CHAPTER 3

Culture and Society

Multiple-Choice Questions

d (page 55)

1. Culture consists of
   a. values.
   b. norms.
   c. material goods.
   d. All of the above
   e. a and b only

b (page 55)

2. The scientific study of culture began with _____ in the nineteenth century.
   a. Marx
   b. Durkheim
   c. Weber
   d. C. Wright Mills
   e. the Internet

c (page 55)

3. Early sociology and anthropology was
   a. unbiased.
   b. biased toward the beliefs and values of non-Western cultures.
   c. biased toward the beliefs and values of highly educated Europeans.
   d. based on the newly discovered work of Chinese scholars.
   e. based on the philosophies of indigenous peoples in the New World.

a (page 55)

4. Values are
   a. abstract ideals.
   b. concrete rules of behavior.
   c. definite principles or rules people are expected to follow.
   d. All of the above
   e. None of the above

c (page 55)

5. Definite principles or rules of behavior people are expected to observe are called
   a. culture.
   b. values.
   c. norms.
   d. material goods.
   e. material bads.

d (page 55)

6. The physical objects a culture creates are known as
   a. culture.
   b. values.
   c. norms.
   d. material goods.
   e. material bads.

d (page 56)

7. A helpful image describing culture is that of
   a. a way of life.
   b. a design for living.
   c. a tool kit of practices, knowledge, and symbols.
   d. All of the above
   e. None of the above

c (page 57)

8. Society is
   a. a set of abstract ideals.
   b. a set of concrete rules of behavior.
   c. a system of interrelationships that connects individuals.
   d. All of the above
   e. None of the above

d (page 56)

9. The concept of "culture" as used by sociologists includes
   a. marriage customs and family life.
   b. the "higher things of the mind" such as art and literature.
   c. material goods made in factories.
   d. All of the above
   e. None of the above

a (page 60)

10. A mother scolds her child for not chewing his pretzels thoroughly. This is an example of
    a. informal social control.
    b. formal social control.
    c. natural selection.
    d. All of the above
    e. None of the above

b (pages 60–61)   11. Because of the recent "cultural turn" in sociology, most
                          sociologists now agree that
                          a.   there is always one correct interpretation of reality in
                               social encounters.
                          b.   different people have different "scripts" in any
                               encounter, and different reasons for choosing one or
                               another.
                          c.   the idea of a "script" is inapplicable to social analysis,
                               since we always just "make it up as we go along."
                          d.   All of the above; sociologists widely disagree on this
                               point.
                          e.   None of the above; the "cultural turn" has nothing to do
                               with day-to-day behavior.

b (page 62)   12. Archaeological evidence suggests the first human culture
                          began about
                          a.   8 million years ago.
                          b.   2 million years ago.
                          c.   800,000 years ago.
                          d.   100,000 years ago.
                          e.   four thousand years ago.

e (page 63)   13. According to sociobiologists, _____ has led to female
                          chastity and male promiscuity.
                          a.   the decay of cultural values
                          b.   cultural relativism
                          c.   ethnocentrism
                          d.   instinct
                          e.   reproductive strategy

e (page 63)   14. Sociobiologists believe
                          a.   that evolution is a theory that does not apply to humans.
                          b.   that much of social life is based in our genetic makeup as
                               human beings.
                          c.   that "reproductive strategy" shapes the relations between
                               the sexes.
                          d.   All of the above
                          e.   b and c only

b (page 64)   15. Human behavior and cultural beliefs
                          a.   are just about the same everywhere.
                          b.   vary widely from culture to culture.
                          c.   are based on instinct.
                          d.   vary only slightly from one culture to another.
                          e.   are based on natural selection.

c (page 63)

16. When it comes to the relationship between nature and nurture in human behavior, sociologists believe that
   a. biology is destiny.
   b. sociology is destiny.
   c. nature and nurture interact to shape human behavior.
   d. All of the above
   e. None of the above

b (page 64)

17. _____ society is culturally diverse, including within it numerous _____.
   a. Hunting and gathering; societies
   b. Industrial; subcultures
   c. Industrial; subsocieties
   d. Hunting and gathering; subsocieties
   e. Human; subspecies

d (page 65)

18. Which of the following could be termed a subculture?
   a. skaters
   b. ravers
   c. vegetarians
   d. All of the above
   e. None of the above; subculture refers only to ethnic or language groups.

d (page 65)

19. Hip-hop is a useful example of
   a. subculture.
   b. multiculturalism.
   c. globalization.
   d. All of the above
   e. None of the above

e (pages 66–67)

20. The Nacirema, subjects of Horace Miner's famous essay on body rituals, are
   a. disgusting.
   b. stupid.
   c. strange.
   d. nonexistent.
   e. American.

a (page 67)

21. Judging other cultures by the standards of one's own is known as
   a. ethnocentrism.
   b. cultural relativism.
   c. nacirema.
   d. macarena.
   e. macaroni.

b (page 67)

22. Assessing a society by its own cultural standards is known as
    a. ethnocentrism.
    b. cultural relativism.
    c. ethnocreationism.
    d. sociobiology.
    e. culturobiology.

d (page 68)

23. Features that are found in virtually all societies are called
    a. cultural relativism.
    b. multiculturalism.
    c. ethnocentrism.
    d. cultural universals.
    e. subcultures.

d (page 68)

24. All cultures possess
    a. language.
    b. some form of family system.
    c. prohibitions against incest.
    d. All of the above
    e. None of the above

d (page 69)

25. The linguistic relativity hypothesis was developed by
    a. Durkheim.
    b. Einstein.
    c. Chomsky.
    d. Sapir and Whorf.
    e. Picard and Riker.

c (pages 71–72)

26. _____ is limited to a particular context; _____ permits transmission of ideas and experiences through many generations and cultures.
    a. Language; culture
    b. Culture; language
    c. Speech; writing
    d. Writing; speech
    e. Culture; society

b (page 72)

27. A _____ is a vehicle of meaning.
    a. chromosome
    b. signifier
    c. tool
    d. society
    e. truck

d (page 72)

28. Which of the following is a signifier?
    a. certain material objects, like dress styles
    b. sounds made in speech
    c. a stop sign
    d. All of the above
    e. None of the above

b (page 72)

29. Semiotics is
    a. the study of premodern societies.
    b. the analysis of nonverbal cultural meanings.
    c. the theory of natural selection.
    d. the use of standardized questionnaires.
    e. the sound of trucks.

a (page 72)

30. In ancient cities, the religious temple was placed in the highest or central location; in modern cities, skyscrapers occupy that position. What method of analysis allows us to compare symbolic cultural meanings of such physical structures?
    a. semiotics
    b. sociobiology
    c. sociophysiology
    d. life history
    e. semiphysics

a (page 73)

31. For most of their existence as a species, humans have lived in
    a. hunting and gathering societies.
    b. pastoral and agrarian societies.
    c. nonindustrial civilizations.
    d. traditional states.
    e. industrial societies.

a (page 74)

32. Very little inequality, no divisions of rich and poor, few differences in power, emphasis on cooperation rather than competition, participatory decision-making, an elaborate ceremonial life; what type of society is described by these characteristics?
    a. hunting and gathering societies
    b. pastoral and agrarian societies
    c. nonindustrial civilizations
    d. traditional states
    e. industrial societies

b (page 74)

33. Which type of society shows that human beings are not simply competitive by nature?
   a. industrial
   b. hunting and gathering
   c. pastoral
   d. agrarian
   e. traditional civilization

b (page 76)

34. _____ societies relied mainly on domesticated animals, while _____ societies grew crops for their livelihood.
   a. Hunting; gathering
   b. Pastoral; agrarian
   c. Agrarian; pastoral
   d. Gathering; hunting
   e. Nonindustrial; industrial

d (page 76)

35. Which type of society is more settled and tends to have more material possessions?
   a. hunting
   b. gathering
   c. pastoral
   d. agrarian
   e. All of the above are equal in those characteristics.

c (page 77)

36. Development of larger cities, pronounced inequality in wealth and power, rule by kings and emperors, written language, flourishing art and science; what type of society exhibits these characteristics?
   a. hunting and gathering societies
   b. pastoral and agrarian societies
   c. nonindustrial civilizations
   d. modern societies
   e. industrial societies

e (page 77)

37. Most of the traditional civilizations were _____, developed through conquest and incorporation of other societies.
   a. hunters and gatherers
   b. pastoral
   c. barbarians
   d. industrial
   e. empires

e (page 77)   38. _____ is the emergence of machine production, based
                      on the use of inanimate power resources.
                      a.   Hunting
                      b.   Pastoral society
                      c.   Agriculture
                      d.   Civilization
                      e.   Industrialization

c (page 77)   39. In which of the following socieities do most people live
                      and work on the land (in agricultural production)?
                      a.   newly industrializing
                      b.   industrialized
                      c.   traditional civilizations
                      d.   All of the above
                      e.   None of the above

e (page 78)   40. A rapid pace of discoveries, inventions, and technological
                      innovation; most people live in cities and work in factories,
                      offices, or shops; social life in the cities is impersonal and
                      many encounters are with strangers; large-scale
                      organizations predominate. What type of society is
                      described by these characteristics?
                      a.   hunting and gathering societies
                      b.   pastoral and agrarian societies
                      c.   nonindustrial civilizations
                      d.   traditional states
                      e.   industrial societies

e (page 79)   41. Which type of society saw the advent of the nation-state?
                      a.   hunting and gathering societies
                      b.   pastoral and agrarian societies
                      c.   nonindustrial civilizations
                      d.   traditional states
                      e.   industrial societies

d (page 79)   42. Political communities with clearly defined borders (rather
                      than vague frontiers) in which the governments have
                      extensive power over citizens' lives are known as
                      a.   barbarian empires.
                      b.   nonindustrial civilizations.
                      c.   traditional states.
                      d.   nation-states.
                      e.   communism.

e (page 79)   43. _____ was the central process shaping the social
                    geography of the modern world.
                    a. Agriculture
                    b. Hunting
                    c. Pastoralism
                    d. Natural selection
                    e. Colonialism

c (page 79)   44. Most societies that were colonies are now
                    a. First World societies.
                    b. Second World societies.
                    c. Developing societies.
                    d. Industrialized societies.
                    e. Post-Industrialized societies.

b (page 79)   45. The First World societies are _____; nearly all have
                    _____ systems of government.
                    a. mostly to the south of the U.S. and Europe; one-party
                    b. industrialized; multiparty
                    c. Communist; one-party
                    d. industrialized; one-party
                    e. Communist; multiparty

b (page 80)   46. Conditions in the developing world today are largely a
                    result of
                    a. their falling behind in the type of development that
                        built the First World.
                    b. colonialism, their contact with Western industrialized
                        societies.
                    c. Communism.
                    d. natural selection.
                    e. their refusal to adopt the nation-state as their political
                        system.

a (page 81)   47. Those developing societies that have begun to successfully
                    develop industrial systems are known as
                    a. newly industrializing economies (NIEs).
                    b. newly First World countries (NFWCs).
                    c. the Second World.
                    d. the Second First World (SFW).
                    e. No Third World societies have been successful in that
                        way.

c (page 81)   48. Of the developing societies undergoing industrialization,
                     which have had the most economic success?
                     a. those in South America
                     b. those in Africa
                     c. those in Asia
                     d. those in Antarctica
                     e. None of them have had economic success.

b (page 82)   49. The industrialized and developing societies have developed
                     a. separately from one another.
                     b. in interconnection with one another.
                     c. at the same rate.
                     d. in entirely different ways, but equally.
                     e. None of the above; the Third World is essentially the
                         same today as it was a thousand years ago.

e (pages 82–83) 50. The variety of products available on store shelves indicate
                     the degree to which the world has become
                     a. dominated by the developing countries.
                     b. dominated by the NIEs.
                     c. separated into isolated nation-states.
                     d. separated by time and space.
                     e. a single, global social system.

d (pages 70–71) 51. Reggae music illustrates the cultural effects of
                     globalization, as it is based on influences from
                     a. West African slaves.
                     b. a religious cult worshipping the late emperor of
                         Ethiopia.
                     c. American rhythm and blues.
                     d. All of the above
                     e. None of the above

b (page 65)   52. Smaller segments of a society with their own unique
                     patterns of behavior are called
                     a. cultural universals.
                     b. subcultures.
                     c. cultural segments.
                     d. colonies.
                     e. subways.

True/False Questions

F (page 65)	1.	Subcultures are groups that are not part of the society.
T (page 55)	2.	The material goods in a culture influence the way of life of its people in significant ways.
F (page 55)	3.	The term culture, as used by sociologists, refers only to things like classical music and art.
F (page 57)	4.	It is possible to have a society without a culture.
T (page 65)	5.	Assimilation is the process by which different cultures are absorbed into a single mainstream culture.
T (page 65)	6.	Multiculturalism acknowledges shared central cultural values while respecting diversity and equality of different cultures.
F (page 72)	7.	The level of material culture in a society completely determines other aspects of cultural development.
T (page 76)	8.	Pastoral and agrarian societies are able to support larger communities than hunting and gathering societies.
F (pages 78–79)	9.	Industrialization was an overwhelmingly peaceful process of development.
F (page 85)	10.	Events in the developing world have little effect on Americans because they are so far away.

Essay Questions

1. Do you agree or disagree with the text's assertion that "most pupils in the United States would be outraged to find another student cheating on an exam"? Discuss this question in terms of your perception of American values and norms.

2. Can cultural norms and values be deliberately changed? If so, how might that happen? Give an example. If not, why not?

3. Discuss how values and norms within a particular society or community might be contradictory. Illustrate using an example from your own culture.

4. Is culture a force for perpetuating values and norms in society or a force for change? Explain.

5. Using hip-hop as an example, discuss the effects of globalization on the formation of subcultures and cultural diversity.

6. Have you ever experienced culture shock? Describe the circumstances using what you have learned about the sociology of culture.

7. Are there any values or norms that could be considered universal? If so, what are they, and what evidence can you cite that they are truly universal? If not, what does this imply about our ability to understand cultures whose values are alien to our own?

8. Discuss the significance of written language for the development of human society.

9. If you could choose one type of pre-modern society to live in, which would you choose? Why? What characteristics of that type of society would you find preferable?

10. Discuss the rise of nationalism in the globalizing world. How do you explain this phenomenon, when globalization seems to lead to homogenization of culture in so many ways? Use the example of Kuwait to illustrate your points.

CHAPTER 4
Socialization and the Life Cycle

Multiple-Choice Questions

b (page 90)

1. The process by which an infant becomes self-aware, knowledgeable, and skilled in the ways of his or her culture is known as
   a. evolution.
   b. socialization.
   c. sensitization.
   d. natural selection.
   e. social interaction.

b (page 90)

2. Children learn the ways of their elders, thereby perpetuating the values, norms, and social practices of their culture. This process is known as
   a. evolution.
   b. socialization.
   c. sensitization.
   d. natural selection.
   e. social interaction.

c (pages 90–92)

3. Cases like those of the "wild boy of Aveyron" and Genie illustrate what a(n) _____ child would be like.
   a. highly evolved
   b. socialized
   c. unsocialized
   d. average
   e. Third World

d (page 92)

4. The examples of "unsocialized" children cited in the text illustrate the fact that _____ is necessary for normal human development.
   a. nature
   b. medicine
   c. psychology
   d. social interaction
   e. None of the above

a (page 92)

5. George Herbert Mead's analysis of child development emphasizes
   a. the emergence of a sense of self.
   b. the stages of cognitive development.
   c. the importance of sociobiology.
   d. All of the above
   e. None of the above

d (page 92)

6. According to George Herbert Mead, children develop a sense of self by
   a. going through distinct stages of sensorimotor development.
   b. going to school and learning to read.
   c. going to church and gaining a soul.
   d. taking the role of the other.
   e. ignoring their parents.

e (page 92)

7. According to George Herbert Mead, the _____ is the unsocialized infant; the _____ is the social self.
   a. ego; superego
   b. id; ego
   c. sensorimotor; concrete operational
   d. me; I
   e. I; me

c (page 93)

8. George Herbert Mead referred to the general morals and values of the culture in which a child develops as the
   a. symbolic morality.
   b. symbolic interaction.
   c. generalized other.
   d. corporalized other.
   e. deputized other.

e (page 92)

9. A child learns to act like adults she observes. Mead refers to this behavior as
   a. "unsocialized".
   b. the "wild child".
   c. preoperational.
   d. the generalized other.
   e. taking the role of the other.

a (page 92)

10. According to Mead, individuals develop self-consciousness by
   a. seeing themselves as others see them.
   b. seeing themselves as the unsocialized infant sees them.
   c. becoming a "wild child".
   d. going through the concrete operational stage.
   e. going through the formal operational stage.

b (page 93)

11. Jean Piaget's theory of child development is based on
   a. the emergence of a sense of self, of self-awareness.
   b. the stages of cognitive development.
   c. the importance of sociobiology.
   d. All of the above
   e. None of the above

d (page 93)

12. From birth to age two, according to Jean Piaget, children are in the _____ stage, in which they learn by touching and manipulating objects.
   a. concrete operational
   b. preoperational
   c. formal operational
   d. sensorimotor
   e. generalized other

b (page 93)

13. The second stage in Jean Piaget's theory, in which children master language and symbolic expression, is called
   a. concrete operational.
   b. preoperational.
   c. formal operational.
   d. sensorimotor.
   e. symbolic interactionism.

a (page 93)

14. From age seven to eleven, children are in Jean Piaget's _____ stage, in which they begin to master abstract, logical ideas like causality.
   a. concrete operational
   b. preoperational
   c. formal operational
   d. sensorimotor
   e. generalized other

c (page 93)

15. Children who reach the _____ stage, usually from age eleven to fifteen, develop the ability to understand highly abstract theory and hypothetical ideas, according to Jean Piaget.
   a. concrete operational
   b. preoperational
   c. formal operational
   d. sensorimotor
   e. generalized other

d (page 94)

16. Groups or social contexts in which significant processes of socialization occur are called
   a. context operations.
   b. concrete operations.
   c. sensorimotors.
   d. agencies of socialization.
   e. agencies of child development.

b (page 94)

17. The most intense period of cultural learning is
   a. formal operational.
   b. primary socialization.
   c. secondary socialization.
   d. generalized other.
   e. young adulthood.

d (page 94)

18. Which of the following is an agency of socialization?
   a. mass media
   b. family
   c. peers
   d. All of the above
   e. None of the above

c (page 95)

19. Which agency of socialization is also the location in which age-based peer groups are formed and reinforced in their impact?
   a. mass media
   b. family
   c. school
   d. All of the above
   e. None of the above

c (pages 95–96)   20. In her book *Gender Play*, Barrie Thorne found significant influence of _____ on gender socialization of children, particularly with respect to their feelings about their developing bodies.
- a. mass media
- b. family
- c. peers
- d. All of the above
- e. None of the above

e (page 97)   21. Which type of television show depicts the highest number of violent acts and episodes?
- a. cop shows
- b. science fiction
- c. talk shows
- d. comedies
- e. cartoons

b (page 97)   22. According to researchers, _____ has the most significant effect on children's behavior.
- a. television violence in itself
- b. the general framework of attitudes in which television violence is presented and "read" (interpreted) by children
- c. the time of day in which violence is portrayed
- d. the age of the violent actors
- e. None of the above; they found no effect whatsoever.

e (page 97)   23. Researchers found that _____ have become a significant part of the culture and socialization of children today, providing a potential distraction from school if other factors are already deflecting interest in schoolwork.
- a. television shows
- b. peer groups
- c. video games
- d. Both a and b
- e. Both a and c

a (page 100)   24. Industrialization brings what big change in work as a
                    socializing process?
                a. Going "out to work" becomes a major transition in a
                    person's life, often requiring important adjustments in
                    attitudes and behavior.
                b. For the first time in history, people have to learn to
                    cooperate with others at work.
                c. Working at home becomes a major part of social life
                    for the first time.
                d. All of the above
                e. None of the above; work is the same in industrialized
                    countries as it always has been.

c (page 100)   25. A person in a particular social position is expected to
                    engage in certain socially defined behaviors. This is his
                a. socialization.
                b. agency.
                c. social role.
                d. peer group.
                e. mature adulthood.

d (page 101)   26. From a sociological persepective, _____ is the source
                    of individuality.
                a. id
                b. ego
                c. gender
                d. socialization
                e. young adulthood

d (page 100)   27. What is *identity*, in the sociological sense?
                a. the understanding of who we are and what is
                    meaningful to us
                b. a set of characteristics we share with others
                c. a set of characteristics that are unique to us as
                    individuals
                d. All of the above
                e. None of the above

a (page 100)   28. Characteristics attributed to an individual by others would
                    be called
                a. social identity.
                b. the "I".
                c. self-identity.
                d. the "me".
                e. peer groups.

a (page 100)

29. Which of the following provides a source of meaning on which a social movement might be built?
    a. social identity
    b. the "I"
    c. self-identity
    d. the "me"
    e. peer groups

c (page 101)

30. The process of self-development through which we establish a unique sense of who we are as a person and our relationship to the rest of the world is known as
    a. social identity.
    b. the "I".
    c. self-identity.
    d. the "me".
    e. peer groups.

b (page 101)

31. The learning of male or female roles takes place through a process called
    a. genderization.
    b. gender socialization.
    c. sexualization.
    d. sex role learning.
    e. taking the role of the gender.

b (page 102)

32. By age _____ children have a partial understanding of what gender is; by age _____ they know that gender does not change.
    a. one; three or four
    b. two; five or six
    c. five; seven or eight
    d. ten; fifteen or sixteen
    e. None of the above; children are born with this knowledge.

d (page 102)

33. Which of the following is a cue to children about appropriate gender behavior for their culture?
    a. nonverbal cues, like different smells of men and women
    b. how they are handled differently by men and women
    c. toys
    d. All of the above
    e. None of the above

a (page 104)   34. Which of the following theories of gender socialization
would be *least* likely to be embraced by feminists?
a.   Freud's
b.   Chodorow's
c.   Gilligan's
d.   All of the above are *equally* likely to be accepted by
feminists.
e.   None of the above is likely to be accepted by
feminists.

c (pages 102–103)   35. In a well-known 1972 study of gender roles in children's
books, Lenore Weitzman and her colleagues found that
a.   the vast majority of the characters were female.
b.   females were more likely to be involved in
adventurous activities.
c.   not a single woman in the books analyzed had a job
outside the home.
d.   All of the above
e.   None of the above

d (page 103)   36. Studies of gender roles in _____ show that most of the
leading figures in active roles are male.
a.   children's books
b.   children's cartoons
c.   commercials on children's television programs
d.   All of the above
e.   None of the above

b (page 103)   37. Why do parents who wish to raise their children in a
nonsexist way have difficulty doing so?
a.   Traditional gender roles are genetically determined.
b.   Traditional gender roles are reproduced in so many
other areas of everyday life.
c.   Parents have no idea what traditional gender roles are.
d.   Parents have no idea how to raise a child in a nonsexist
way.
e.   No parents really want to raise their children in a
nonsexist way.

d (page 106)   38. The stages of the human life course are
a.   biological.
b.   social.
c.   influenced by culture.
d.   All of the above
e.   None of the above

d (pages 106–107) 39. Before the twentieth century, at what stage in the life course did people do productive work for their families or others?
    a. childhood
    b. teens
    c. young adulthood
    d. All of the above
    e. None of the above; people didn't work until they reached mature adulthood.

b (page 107) 40. Age-grades facilitate
    a. gender identity formation.
    b. negotiation of psychosexual development.
    c. equality across the life course.
    d. All of the above
    e. None of the above

b (page 107) 41. _____ is a period of personal and sexual development that seems to be growing in importance.
    a. Childhood
    b. Young adulthood
    c. Mature adulthood
    d. All of the above
    e. None of the above

c (pages 107–108) 42. Which stage of the life course in modern society involves greater individual freedom and responsibility, which may produce a "midlife crisis" for those who feel they have missed opportunities?
    a. childhood
    b. young adulthood
    c. mature adulthood
    d. All of the above
    e. None of the above

e (page 109) 43. The highest status in traditional cultures was the age grade of
    a. childhood.
    b. teenager.
    c. young adulthood.
    d. mature adulthood.
    e. elder.

d (page 109)   44. In _____ societies, elders often lack authority within
the family and community.
a. traditional
b. medieval
c. pastoral
d. industrialized
e. hunting and gathering

d (page 94)   45. Socialization provides an individual with
a. values.
b. behavioral guidelines.
c. the capacity for independent thought and free will.
d. All of the above
e. None of the above

b (pages 93–94)   46. Learning the fixed, more or less rigid rules of _____
gives us the ability to know ourselves and gain some degree
of creative control over our lives.
a. locomotion
b. language
c. age-grades
d. life course
e. solitaire

a (page 92)   47. In George Herbert Mead's theory of socialization,
_____ is accomplished when individuals see
themselves as others see them.
a. self-consciousness
b. other-consciousness
c. selfishness
d. the sensorimotor stage
e. Nirvana

c (page 95)   48. Social groups with similar age and social background are
known as
a. age-groups.
b. socializing groups.
c. peer groups.
d. peer-grades.
e. social grades.

b (page 95)

49. Formalized peer groups are known as
    a. age-groups.
    b. age-grades.
    c. peer groups.
    d. peer-grades.
    e. social grades.

c (page 104)

50. Sigmund Freud's theory of gender development is based on the presence or absence of a
    a. mother.
    b. father.
    c. penis.
    d. vagina.
    e. mind.

b (page 104)

51. Sigmund Freud assumes the _____ is the main source of discipline for the child, creating fear of this person, especially for boys.
    a. mother
    b. father
    c. aunt
    d. uncle
    e. church

a (page 104)

52. Nancy Chodorow's theory of gender development is based on the work of _____, though she places primary emphasis on the development of femininity rather than masculinity.
    a. Sigmund Freud
    b. George Herbert Mead
    c. Karl Marx
    d. Émile Durkheim
    e. Max Weber

a (page 104)

53. Nancy Chodorow's theory of gender development emphasizes the emotional attachment of the child to its _____ as key to its development, which takes place differently for boys than for girls.
    a. mother
    b. father
    c. aunt
    d. uncle
    e. church

b (page 105)

54. Why are women more sensitive and compassionate than men, according to Nancy Chodorow's theory of gender development?
    a. they have penis envy, which makes them sympathetic
    b. they are able to stay emotionally and physically closer to their mother
    c. they are molded by cultural agents such as the media to be that way
    d. All of the above
    e. None of the above

a (page 105)

55. According to Nancy Chodorow's theory of gender development, men are more analytical and manipulative because
    a. they gain a sense of self by making a radical rejection of their closeness to their mothers.
    b. they are driven by the presence of male hormones in their bloodstream.
    c. they fear their fathers.
    d. All of the above
    e. None of the above

d (page 105)

56. Carol Gilligan's research on gender roles suggests women are socialized to find success in _____ rather than _____.
    a. sex; money
    b. money; sex
    c. morality; rewards
    d. helping others; their own individual achievements
    e. their own individual achievements; helping others

b (page 108)

57. In premodern Japan the transition between childhood and adulthood was part of _____ and took place through _____.
    a. politics; voting
    b. an age-grade system; a special rite
    c. work; promotion by managers
    d. All of the above
    e. None of the above

a (page 108)   58. Norms emphasizing _____ were especially strong in
                     premodern Japan.
                     a.   duties of children toward their parents
                     b.   sexual promiscuity
                     c.   the need for experimentation during the teen years
                     d.   All of the above
                     e.   None of the above

c (pages 108–109) 59. In her comparative study of Japanese and American
                       teenagers, Mary White found
                       a.   a great deal of rebellion among both groups.
                       b.   the Americans were more rebellious than the Japanese.
                       c.   a great amount of conformity and respect for parents in
                            both cultures.
                       d.   All of the above
                       e.   None of the above

d (page 109)   60. What is a key difference between Japanese and American
                     teenagers?
                     a.   The Japanese are ahead in academic achievement.
                     b.   The Japanese teens stay closer to their parents than the
                          Americans.
                     c.   The American teens put sex at the top of their
                          priorities.
                     d.   All of the above
                     e.   None of the above

d (page 109)   61. When it comes to sex, Japanese teenagers
                     a.   are very active.
                     b.   separate physical passion from socially approved
                          marriage and romance.
                     c.   tend not to combine it with dating.
                     d.   All of the above
                     e.   None of the above

True/False Questions

T (page 90)   1. Social reproduction is made possible by socialization.

T (page 94)   2. Not all adults have accomplished the formal operational
                     stage, according to Jean Piaget.

T (page 94)   3. The family is the main socializing agency in all cultures.

F (pages 94–95)   4. In *all* cultures, adult relatives other than a child's parents are rarely involved in the child's socialization.

T (pages 101–102)   5. Research shows that adults react differently toward a child depending on what sex they think it is.

T (page 106)   6. The concept of childhood as a distinct phase of life between infancy and teenage did not arise until the last two or three centuries.

T (page 107)   7. Childhood as a separate stage is diminishing due to early exposure to such socializing experiences as adult television shows.

F (page 90)   8. Socialization is a process in which culture stamps people into molds, ultimately undermining their individuality and free will.

F (page 104)   9. Sigmund Freud's theory of socialization has been criticized because it fails to consider the sexual feelings of boys toward their mothers.

F (page 106)   10. The stages of the life course are pretty much the same no matter which culture or time period you look at.

Essay Questions

1. Using your favorite novel of childhood, discuss the process of socialization as it is portrayed by the characters in the book.

2. Why are "unsocialized" children—like the "wild boy of Aveyron" or Genie—unable to exhibit "normal" human behavior?

3. Compare the child development theories of G. H. Mead and Jean Piaget. Which one focuses more on the importance of social interaction in socialization? Explain.

4. Of all the agencies of socialization, which do you think is most influential in childhood? Over the life course of the individual? Explain.

5. Do peer groups take the form of age-grades in your society? If so, what are the age-grades, and how are they involved in socialization? If not, what is the relationship between age and peer-group formation? What agencies of socialization are involved?

6. Discuss the role of the mass media as an agent of socialization. What type of social identity is promoted? How is this behavior reinforced? Is it effective? How do you know?

7. Is the Internet an agency of socialization? If so, in what ways? If not, why not?

8. Is gender innate or learned? Cite specific research to support your position.

9. What, if any, sociological value can be found in Freud's theory of gender socialization?

10. Compare the teenage stage of the life course for Japanese and American youth. How do you account for the similarities and differences?

CHAPTER 5
Social Interaction and Everyday Life

Multiple-Choice Questions

c (page 114)

1. Two people walking on a city sidewalk quickly glance at each other then look away as they pass. Erving Goffman called this type of interaction
   a. the look.
   b. the glance.
   c. civil inattention.
   d. uncivil behavior.
   e. rude.

e (page 114)

2. When a person uses civil inattention with another person, he or she is indicating
   a. hostility.
   b. evil intent.
   c. a warning to the other person.
   d. All of the above
   e. None of the above

d (page 114)

3. Holding the direct gaze of another (staring into his or her eyes)
   a. is usually only done with a lover, a close friend or acquaintance, or a family member.
   b. may be taken as an indicator of hostility.
   c. may be taken as a sign of mistrust.
   d. All of the above
   e. None of the above

b (page 114)

4. Nonintrusive recognition of others, done more or less unconsciously, is called
   a. social interaction.
   b. civil inattention.
   c. sociological imagination.
   d. social recognition.
   e. sleepwalking.

d (pages 114–115)   5. The study of everyday life shows
    a. how behavior is shaped and guided by social forces like roles and norms.
    b. how individuals shape their social reality, including social forces like roles and norms.
    c. how individual behavior is neither fixed nor unstructured.
    d. All of the above
    e. None of the above

a (page 116)   6. Which of the following statements is *true?*
    a. Infants have facial expressions similar to those of adults.
    b. Even the nuances of a smile—how long it lasts, for example—are the same in every culture.
    c. Certain gestures—like thumbs up, for example—mean the same thing everywhere.
    d. All of the above
    e. None of the above

b (page 116)   7. If a man stares at a woman his attitude is likely perceived as innocent; if a woman stares at a man, she is likely seen as inviting. This difference in meaning is
    a. natural.
    b. one way gender inequality is reinforced.
    c. one way gender equality is reinforced.
    d. meaningless.
    e. imaginary.

d (page 117)   8. The meaning of expressions in a conversation depends on
    a. the words.
    b. the sentences.
    c. the social context.
    d. All of the above
    e. None of the above

d (pages 114–115)   9. Studying day-to-day interactions is important because
    a. they make up the bulk of our social activities.
    b. they give structure to what we do.
    c. they shed light on larger institutions and systems.
    d. All of the above
    e. None of the above

---

a (page 115)

10. Nonverbal communication is
    a. the exchange of information and meaning through facial expressions, gestures, and movements of the body.
    b. sometimes referred to as ESP.
    c. really just a myth, as all communication ultimately requires words.
    d. All of the above
    e. None of the above

b (page 115)

11. Paul Ekman and colleagues devised a method for studying nonverbal communication called FACS, or
    a. Fairly Accurate Coding System.
    b. Facial Action Coding System.
    c. Factual Area Correlation Scheme.
    d. Fancy And Creative Seeing.
    e. Family And Children Sharing.

b (page 115)

12. Charles Darwin believed that basic human emotional expressions _____; Paul Ekman's research _____ this view.
    a. are innate and the same in all human beings; refutes
    b. are innate and the same in all human beings; supports
    c. vary widely; refutes
    d. vary widely; supports
    e. None of the above; Darwin had no view on this issue.

c (page 115)

13. As a form of social interaction, the exchange of information and meaning through facial expressions, gestures, and movements of the body is called
    a. ethnomethodology.
    b. saving face.
    c. nonverbal communication.
    d. unfocused interaction.
    e. the compulsion of proximity.

c (page 117)

14. Ethnomethodology is
    a. the nonintrusive recognition of others, done more or less unconsciously.
    b. the process by which we act and react to others around us.
    c. the study of folk or lay methods people use to make sense of what others say and do.
    d. All of the above
    e. None of the above

b (page 117)

15. The founder of ethnomethodology was
    a. Erving Goffman.
    b. Harold Garfinkel.
    c. Paul Simon.
    d. George Herbert Mead.
    e. Émile Durkheim.

a (page 117)

16. An ethnomethodologist would likely study
    a. the underlying social context of seemingly trivial everyday talk and conversations.
    b. the economic factors leading to major wars.
    c. the political systems of traditional empires.
    d. All of the above
    e. None of the above

c (page 117)

17. An ethnomethodologist would study all of the following EXCEPT
    a. conversations in a café.
    b. casual greetings.
    c. gender socialization.
    d. talk.
    e. rules of everyday conversation.

b (page 117)

18. _____, founded by Harold Garfinkel, studies "talk" and "conversation," or the ways in which we actively make sense of what others say or do.
    a. Ethnography
    b. Ethnomethodology
    c. Symbolic studies
    d. Communications
    e. Microsociology

c (pages 117–118)

19. Harold Garfinkel conducted experiments in which students were encouraged to pursue the precise meaning of general or casual comments. The intent was to uncover the _____ that people use to structure and organize everyday conversation.
    a. formal grammar
    b. deceptive tactics
    c. background expectancies
    d. facial expressions
    e. political motives

b (page 117)

20. Communicating through plain, everyday language requires
    a. conscious attention to the rules of formal grammar.
    b. an array of complex, shared background understandings.
    c. an intimate knowledge of the personalities involved in the conversation.
    d. All of the above
    e. None of the above

d (page 119)

21. The technique used by Duneier and Molotch to compare interactions between street people and passersby in New York City was
    a. survey analysis.
    b. comparative historical analysis.
    c. life history.
    d. conversation analysis.
    e. semiotics.

e (page 119)

22. A male street person repeatedly tries to initiate conversation with a female upper class person, despite her obvious unwillingness to respond. This is an example of
    a. FACS.
    b. ethnomethodology.
    c. civil inattention.
    d. response cries.
    e. interactional vandalism.

d (page 122)

23. True story: The Japanese exchange student dropped a spoon on the floor as she carried her dish to the kitchen. As the spoon clattered loudly on the tile floor she exclaimed, "Ooooooh, sorry!" This is an example of a
    a. facial expression.
    b. personal space.
    c. slip of the tongue.
    d. response cry.
    e. None of the above; it was just a simple reflex.

b (page 122)

24. The purpose of response cries, according to Erving Goffman, is
    a. to express the person's unconscious motivations.
    b. to show others one's continued competence in daily routines.
    c. to get others to feel sorry for one's failures.
    d. All of the above
    e. None of the above

a (page 123)

25. When people are in the presence of others—like at a party—and show awareness of each other nonverbally, without talking directly, they are engaged in
    a. unfocused interaction.
    b. focused interaction.
    c. response cries.
    d. slips of the tongue.
    e. deviant behavior.

b (page 123)

26. When people directly attend to what others are saying or doing they are engaged in
    a. unfocused interaction.
    b. focused interaction.
    c. response cries.
    d. slips of the tongue.
    e. deviant behavior.

e (page 123)

27. Erving Goffman refers to an instance of focused interaction as
    a. a response cry.
    b. a slip of the tongue.
    c. unfocused interaction.
    d. deviant behavior.
    e. an encounter.

d (page 123)

28. Which of the following would be an example of an encounter?
    a. a brief conversation with a waiter about the weather
    b. a class discussion
    c. a small group sharing a bottle of wine at a party
    d. All of the above
    e. None of the above

d (page 123)

29. In studying social interaction, what happens in an "opening"?
    a. civil inattention is discarded
    b. a risk of misunderstanding is taken
    c. an encounter is initiated
    d. All of the above
    e. None of the above

c (page 123)

30. Which of the following would *not* be a case in which both focused and unfocused interaction are likely to occur?
    a. a lunchtime crowd in a university cafeteria
    b. the parking lot before a football game
    c. an individual standing alone in a library
    d. All of the above
    e. None of the above

b (page 123)

31. Sometimes a person will smile, but an observer notes that the person's eyes look sad. Goffman would say the sad eyes are part of the expressions the person
    a. gives.
    b. gives off.
    c. manages.
    d. focuses.
    e. None of the above; Goffman is not interested in such details of social interaction.

b (page 123)

32. Why do people use impression management?
    a. They want to protect personal space.
    b. They are sensitive about how others see them.
    c. They want to be good actors.
    d. They prefer impression management over unfocused interactions.
    e. None of the above

b (page 123)

33. Socially defined expectations of a person in a given social position are referred to as
    a. a status.
    b. a social role.
    c. markers.
    d. response cries.
    e. brackets.

e (page 123)

34. Erving Goffman uses the term _____ to refer to the ways people try to shape the reactions of others to themselves.
    a. social positioning
    b. civil inattention
    c. brackets
    d. social rolling
    e. impression management

a (page 123)

35. Another term for social position is
   a. social status.
   b. social role.
   c. marker.
   d. bracket.
   e. social impression.

d (page 124)

36. A person occupies many social positions in various social contexts. This group of statuses that a person holds is (are) called
   a. social positions.
   b. brackets.
   c. occupation.
   d. status set.
   e. status context.

d (page 124)

37. A status one is assigned based on biological factors is referred to as
   a. social role.
   b. assigned role.
   c. master status.
   d. ascribed status.
   e. achieved status.

e (page 124)

38. A status that is earned through the person's own effort is called
   a. social role.
   b. assigned role.
   c. master status.
   d. ascribed status.
   e. achieved status.

c (page 124)

39. A status that has priority over all others and which determines a person's overall position in society is known as
   a. social role.
   b. assigned role.
   c. master status.
   d. ascribed status.
   e. achieved status.

c (page 124)

40. In almost every case, a person's race would be a(n)
   a. role.
   b. achieved status.
   c. ascribed status.
   d. front region.
   e. back region.

d (page 124)   41. According to the text, which of the following would be a
                       master status in modern society?
                       a.   race
                       b.   class
                       c.   gender
                       d.   *a* and *c*
                       e.   All of the above

d (page 124)   42. Erving Goffman referred to those occasions in which people
                       act out formal roles, as if they were on stage, as
                       a.   social roles.
                       b.   master statuses.
                       c.   social positions.
                       d.   front regions.
                       e.   back regions.

e (page 124)   43. Erving Goffman referred to those occasions where people
                       can relax and prepare themselves for more formal
                       interactions as
                       a.   social roles.
                       b.   master statuses.
                       c.   social positions.
                       d.   front regions.
                       e.   back regions.

d (page 129)   44. Forms of electronic communication such as chat rooms,
                       e-mail, and instant messaging have the *disadvantage* of
                       a.   increasing indirect, rather than direct, interaction.
                       b.   increasing the isolation of individuals.
                       c.   hiding the cues we get from other people's faces and
                            bodies in face-to-face communication.
                       d.   All of the above
                       e.   None of the above

c (page 129)   45. Forms of electronic communication such as e-mail, chat
                       rooms, and instant messaging have the *advantage* of
                       a.   increasing direct, rather than indirect, interaction.
                       b.   increasing the isolation of individuals.
                       c.   hiding markers that might indicate a subordinate status,
                            so that people can focus on the content of the message
                            rather than the status of the messenger.
                       d.   All of the above
                       e.   None of the above

b (page 134)   46. Elijah Anderson's study of everyday life in two adjacent
                      urban neighborhoods showed that tensions in social
                      interaction are often based on
                      a.   the deviant personalities of individuals involved.
                      b.   stereotypes about the presumed statuses of the
                           individuals involved.
                      c.   conversation between those involved.
                      d.   All of the above
                      e.   None of the above

d (page 134)   47. Which of the following behavioral cues are used by people
                      encountering strangers on the street to assess the possibility
                      of threat, according to Elijah Anderson's research?
                      a.   skin color
                      b.   gender
                      c.   age
                      d.   All of the above
                      e.   None of the above

e (page 126)   48. Which zone of personal space is within one-and-a-half feet
                      and is reserved for relationships in which regular touching
                      of the body is permitted?
                      a.   touching distance
                      b.   public distance
                      c.   social distance
                      d.   personal distance
                      e.   intimate distance

c (page 126)   49. Which zone of personal space, between four and twelve
                      feet, is that used in formal situations like an interview?
                      a.   touching distance
                      b.   public distance
                      c.   social distance
                      d.   personal distance
                      e.   intimate distance

b (page 126)   50. Which zone of personal space is beyond twelve feet and
                      used by someone speaking to an audience?
                      a.   touching distance
                      b.   public distance
                      c.   social distance
                      d.   personal distance
                      e.   intimate distance

d (page 126)   51. Which zone of personal space is normally used by friends
                        and close acquaintances and extends from one-and-a-half
                        to four feet?
                        a.   touching distance
                        b.   public distance
                        c.   social distance
                        d.   personal distance
                        e.   intimate distance

b (page 126)   52. The concept of _____ refers to how social life is
                        organized in time and space.
                        a.   impression management
                        b.   regionalization
                        c.   time-space convergence
                        d.   social constructionism
                        e.   symbolic interaction

c (page 132)   53. A theoretical perpective which involves the analysis of the
                        processes by which people come to perceive what is "real"
                        to them in social life is called
                        a.   functionalism.
                        b.   Marxism.
                        c.   social constructionism.
                        d.   All of the above
                        e.   None of the above

True/False Questions

F (page 114)   1. Civil inattention is another term for the "hate stare" that
                        was used in the past to intimidate African Americans.

T (page 114)   2. The study of social interaction in everyday life is
                        meaningful because our daily routines give structure and
                        form important patterns in our existence.

F (page 115)   3. The study of social interaction in everyday life reveals
                        nothing significant about the social system as a whole;
                        large-scale systems must be studied separately.

F (page 115)   4. Paul Ekman found that basic facial expressions for
                        emotions like happiness or sadness were different from one
                        culture to another.

T (page 116) 5. There are no gestures or postures of the body that are characteristic in all cultures.

T (page 116) 6. The underlying conventions of everyday talk and conversation are fundamental to the very fabric of social life.

T (page 126) 7. People tend to engage in regionalization, the process of organizing their daily social life in specific zones of time and space.

F (page 127) 8. Clock time is simply a traditional standard and is really unnecessary for modern social life.

F (pages 128–129) 9. Unlike the !Kung, people in modern society have no "compulsion of proximity" and could conduct all interaction indirectly, such as over the phone or Internet.

F (page 133) 10. Microsociology and macrosociology are not connected in any way.

Essay Questions

1. Sociologists talk about how our daily interactions with others result in the social construction of our social reality. Explain what this means, and illustrate the process using a detailed example.

2. Is nonverbal communication innate, cultural, or both? Explain, using examples and citing specific research to support your position.

3. What are "background expectancies"? What role do they play in conversation? In the processes and structures of everyday life?

4. What is "interactional vandalism"? Describe the case of Mudrick and the women passersby in Duneier and Molotch's 1999 study. Why does interactional vandalism create problems in everyday interaction and conversation?

5. Describe a situation in which you have engaged in both unfocused and focused interaction with others. Discuss the encounter from beginning to end, making sure to employ the appropriate terms used by Goffman and other sociologists to analyze such situations.

6. Describe your status set. Which of these statuses are ascribed? Which are achieved? Which is your master status? Be sure to indicate why each status fits in its category.

7. Imagine living in a world that does not function by clock time. How would your everyday activities be different? Could you maintain your current way of life in such conditions? If so, how? If not, why not?

8. What is social constructionism? What do Berger and Luckmann mean by the "social construction of reality"? How do social constructionists examine social life? Give an example.

9. What is the "compulsion of proximity"? How is it affected by technologies such as the Internet?

10. Describe an encounter you have had in a cultural context that differs from the one in which you live. How was the social interaction different from what you are familiar with in your everyday life? Discuss issues such as nonverbal communication, personal space, gestures, eye contact, stereotypes, time, and space.

CHAPTER 6

Groups, Networks, and Organizations

Multiple-Choice Questions

a (page 138)

1. Which of the following is a *social group?*
   a. an unmarried couple
   b. you and all other people like you
   c. people waiting at Terminal C for flight 181
   d. All of the above
   e. None of the above

c (page 139)

2. Which of the following is a *social aggregate?*
   a. an unmarried couple
   b. you and all other people like you
   c. people waiting at Terminal C for flight 181
   d. All of the above
   e. None of the above

b (page 139)

3. Bert is a New York Yankees fan. To Bert, Boston Red Sox fans are an
   a. in-group.
   b. out-group.
   c. aggregate.
   d. All of the above
   e. None of the above

a (page 139)

4. Which is more likely to be an in-group?
   a. primary group
   b. secondary group
   c. social aggregate
   d. social category
   e. None of the above

a (page 140)

5. Which of the following is true?
   a. A person measures his or her own worth by the standards of a reference group.
   b. One must belong to a group for it to be one's reference group.
   c. Reference groups are always primary groups.
   d. All of the above
   e. None of the above

b (page 141)

6. A group consisting of two people is known as a
   a. monad.
   b. dyad.
   c. triad.
   d. doodad.
   e. wantad.

c (page 144)

7. In Milgram's study about _____, over half the subjects were willing to follow a scientist's orders even to the point of apparent pain or death of another participant.
   a. networks
   b. groupthink
   c. obedience to authority
   d. transactional leaders
   e. reference groups

d (page 146)

8. Which of the following is true regarding social *networks?*
   a. It's not *what* you know, it's *who* you know.
   b. Not all networks are social groups.
   c. The Bohemian Grove is an elite network.
   d. All of the above
   e. None of the above

e (page 149)

9. What term do sociologists use to refer to a group with an identifiable membership that engages in concerted collective actions to achieve a common purpose?
   a. primary group
   b. secondary group
   c. in-group
   d. out-group
   e. organization

d (page 148)   10. Formal organizations
                                   a.   are rationally designed to achieve their objectives.
                                   b.   often employ explicit rules, regulations, and procedures.
                                   c.   have risen to prominence in modern societies largely due to their legal stature.
                                   d.   All of the above
                                   e.   None of the above

b (page 148)   11. A large grouping of people that engages in concerted collective actions to achieve specific objectives is called
                                   a.   an oligarchy.
                                   b.   an organization.
                                   c.   a primary group.
                                   d.   All of the above
                                   e.   None of the above

b (page 149)   12. People in modern societies depend on _____ to take care of everything from how we are born, to our daily supply of running water, even to the way we die.
                                   a.   nature
                                   b.   organizations
                                   c.   the spiritual world
                                   d.   tradition
                                   e.   primary groups

e (page 149)   13. Which of the following is an example of an organization?
                                   a.   a hospital
                                   b.   the phone company
                                   c.   the utility company
                                   d.   a prison
                                   e.   All of the above

c (page 149)   14. The first systematic interpretation of modern organizations was developed by
                                   a.   Émile Durkheim.
                                   b.   Karl Marx.
                                   c.   Max Weber.
                                   d.   Michel Foucault.
                                   e.   Alexis de Tocqueville.

a (page 149)

15 All large organizations tend to be _____, according to Max Weber.
    a. bureaucracies
    b. primary groups
    c. inefficient
    d. All of the above
    e. None of the above

b (page 149)

16. The word "bureaucracy," as coined by Monsieur de Gournay, literally means
    a. terrible organization.
    b. the rule of officials.
    c. large table.
    d. people are furniture.
    e. rule by pipsqueaks.

b (page 150)

17. Max Weber believed _____ was the only way to cope with the administrative needs of large social systems.
    a. tradition
    b. bureaucracy
    c. surveillance
    d. emotion
    e. charismatic authority

c (page 150)

18. According to Max Weber's, term "ideal type of bureaucracy" refers to what?
    a. the most desirable kind
    b. the easiest font to read, best for using in bureaucratic records
    c. an abstract description constructed by accentuating certain features of real cases in order to reveal their most important characteristics
    d. All of the above
    e. None of the above

e (page 150)

19. Which of the following is among the characteristics of Max Weber's ideal type of bureaucracy?
    a. Ownership is not in the hands of the workers.
    b. There is a complete separation between work and home life.
    c. Each job has a definite and fixed salary attached to it.
    d. A set of rules governs the conduct of officials at all levels of the organization.
    e. All of the above

b (page 150)

20. Regarding bureaucracies, Max Weber concluded that the closer they were to the ideal type, the more _____ they would become.
   a. ineffective in achieving their objectives
   b. effective in achieving their objectives
   c. loose and informal
   d. like a feudal estate
   e. like a democracy

a (page 150)

21. Max Weber likened bureaucracies to _____ operating on the principle of _____.
   a. machines; rationality
   b. organisms; evolution
   c. men; emotionalism
   d. rivers; erosion
   e. None of the above

a (page 150)

22. The relations between people as stated in the rules of an organization are
   a. formal relations.
   b. informal relations.
   c. primary groups.
   d. surveillance.
   e. flexible.

b (page 150)

23. Peter Blau studied _____ in a government agency, the ways of doing things that allowed more flexibility than was possible within the formal structure of the bureaucracy.
   a. formal relations
   b. informal relations
   c. secondary groups
   d. official rules
   e. surveillance

a (page 151)

24. John Meyer and Brian Rowan found that the _____ in a bureaucracy are often ceremonial or ritual, serving mainly to justify the way things are really done.
   a. formal procedures
   b. informal relations
   c. primary groups
   d. traditions
   e. surveillance systems

d (page 152)   25. In the popular movie *John Doe,* a hospital administrator
refuses to approve a child's operation because his father's
insurance policy has recently been changed. Merton would
refer to such strict adherence to the rules as
a.   the ideal type bureaucracy.
b.   formal organization.
c.   functional.
d.   bureaucratic ritualism.
e.   bureaucratic surveillance.

c (page 153)   26. Michel Foucault showed that the physical architecture
occupied by an organization reflects its
a.   level of debt.
b.   age.
c.   system of authority.
d.   All of the above
e.   None of the above

d (page 153)   27. Michel Foucault's term for the supervision of activities in
organizations is
a.   power.
b.   bureaucracy.
c.   democracy.
d.   surveillance.
e.   the clan model.

b (page 154)   28. According to Michel Foucault, organizations "efficiently
distribute bodies" and activities through the use of
a.   democracy.
b.   timetables.
c.   the clan model.
d.   All of the above
e.   None of the above

d (pages 153–154) 29. Which of the following resemble prisons in their use of
physical separation and surveillance to maximize control
over individuals, according to Michel Foucault?
a.   factories
b.   schools
c.   hospitals
d.   All of the above
e.   None of the above

c (page 154)   30. Michel Foucault referred to Jeremy Bentham's model of
the _____ as the image of the modern organization, in
which surveillance plays a central role.
a. clan model
b. bureaucracy
c. Panopticon
d. Peter Pan icon
e. insane asylum

d (page 154)   31. Some analysts conclude that we now live in a _____, in
which information about our lives is gathered by all kinds
of organizations.
a. clan model
b. iron law of oligarchy
c. Panopticon
d. surveillance society
e. insane asylum

c (page 172)   32. What is the main reason Americans participate less in civic
activities now than they did in the past, according to Robert
Putnam?
a. bowling leagues
b. traffic jams
c. television
d. the Bohemian Grove
e. the Internet

b (page 155)   33. What is the term for "rule by the few"?
a. clan model
b. oligarchy
c. Panopticon
d. democracy
e. surveillance

b (page 155)   34. Robert Michels saw that in large-scale organizations, and
in societies dominated by such organizations, power
inevitably concentrated at the top. He called this the
a. clan model.
b. iron law of oligarchy.
c. Panopticon.
d. surveillance society.
e. insane asylum.

b (pages 157–159)   35. Judy Wajcman's analysis of women in management
                         suggests that existing organizations are "thoroughly
                         gendered" in their managerial structure. In this respect, her
                         analysis reinforces the _____ approach used by Kathy
                         Ferguson in *The Feminist Case Against Bureaucracy*.
                         a.   liberal feminist
                         b.   radical feminist
                         c.   bureaucratic ritualist
                         d.   social capitalist
                         e.   None of the above

a (page 160)   36. How do Japanese corporations differ from the Weberian
                         model followed by most business organizations in the
                         West?
                         a.   Japanese corporations use bottom-up decision making,
                              rather than a pyramidal hierarchy of authority.
                         b.   Employees in Japanese corporations specialize more.
                         c.   There is less job security in Japan.
                         d.   Japanese employees are more individualistic than their
                              Western counterparts.
                         e.   The Japanese maintain a strict separation between
                              work and their private lives.

b (page 161)   37. Comparing Japanese corporations with Max Weber's
                         model of bureaucracy, William Ouchi concluded that the
                         _____ model was more efficient.
                         a.   bureaucratic
                         b.   clan
                         c.   formal
                         d.   Western
                         e.   American

c (page 161)   38. A company invents its own mascot and song, which is sung
                         by employees at the beginning of each shift. This style is
                         known as
                         a.   song and dance management.
                         b.   human resources management.
                         c.   corporate culture.
                         d.   socialism.
                         e.   corporatism.

a (page 162)

39. _____ is changing the face of many organizations, allowing them to avoid layoffs by allowing workers to _____, working from home as independent contractors.
    a. Information technology; telecommute
    b. Bureaucracy; be McDonaldized
    c. Surveillance; be monitored
    d. The clan system; escape the clan
    e. None of the above; no one really works from home any more.

b (page 162)

40. The increasing use of "high-tech" in the workplace is leading to the development of _____ of workers.
    a. one big class
    b. two classes
    c. three distinct classes
    d. infinite classes
    e. no classes

a (page 163)

41. What is disintegrating in the globalized economy, according to Manuel Castells?
    a. traditional bureaucracy
    b. networks
    c. large corporations
    d. All of the above
    e. None of the above

b (page 163)

42. Strategic alliances formed among the largest corporations for the purpose of planning production and managing problems are known as
    a. network enterprises.
    b. enterprise webs.
    c. World Wide Webs.
    d. corporate socialism.
    e. social corporatism.

e (page 168)

43. Which of the following is an advantage of networked organizations over traditional formal bureaucracies?
    a. Networked organizations are more hierarchical, permitting more efficient decision making.
    b. Networked organizations are more decentralized, allowing a freer flow of information.
    c. Networked organizations permit more creativity in problem solving.
    d. _a_ and _b_
    e. _b_ and _c_

b (page 169)   44. Which of the following is an international governmental
                    organization?
                    a.   the Bohemian Grove
                    b.   the European Union
                    c.   the International Planned Parenthood Federation
                    d.   the International Sociological Association
                    e.   the International Committee to Ban Land Mines

d (page 170)   45. Which type of organization is established by agreements
                    among its individual members and private organizations?
                    a.   the Bohemian Grove
                    b.   a social aggregate
                    c.   a secondary group
                    d.   an international nongovernmental organization
                    e.   an international governmental organization

d (page 168)   46. According to George Ritzer, the principles of rationality
                    that guide the McDonald's fast-food restaurant chain are
                    increasingly being adopted by other organizations in
                    American society and throughout the world. Which of the
                    following is among those principles?
                    a.   efficiency
                    b.   uniformity
                    c.   control through automation
                    d.   All of the above
                    e.   None of the above

True/False Questions

T (page 139)   1. Two people can be a social group.

F (page 149)   2. The influence of organizations over our lives today is
                    entirely beneficial.

T (page 153)   3. Modern organizations tend to occupy buildings that share
                    common architectural characteristics with buildings of
                    other organizations, no matter what the type of
                    organization.

F (page 153)   4. The higher the position in an organization, the more the behavior of the person is under surveillance, according to Foucault.

T (page 154)   5. The maintenance of written and computerized records by modern organizations is a form of subtle surveillance.

F (page 155)   6. History has shown that organizations and societies based on high levels of surveillance are most efficient.

F (page 160)   7. Japanese corporations are good examples of the bureaucratic model outlined by Weber.

F (page 160)   8. Studies show that Western companies cannot successfully operate with the kind of bottom-up decision making used in Japan.

F (page 160)   9. The bottom-up decision making style has not been found to work in Western societies.

T (page 161)   10. Human resource management (HRM) is a style that sees human resources issues as the responsibility of the whole organization, not just the Human Resources department.

Essay Questions

1. How would you explain the behavior of people in groups like Heaven's Gate? Be sure to use sociological concepts and theories dealing with groups, conformity, and technology in formulating your essay.

2. Cooley worried about the loss of intimacy as secondary groups became more prominent and pervasive. Durkheim and Simmel saw some benefits to the development of more secondary groups. What do you think about the trend toward more secondary group relationships in modern society?

3. Compare the dynamics of dyads, triads, and larger groups. In which groups are the relationships more intense? Which are more stable? Why?

4. Give an example of each of the following from your own experience or from your knowledge of history: a) transformational leader; b) transactional leader. What did each person do that fit that particular category?

5. Compare the findings of Asch, Milgram, and Janis regarding conformity. Why did the subjects respond the way they did in each of these studies?

6. What is groupthink? Why does it occur? What are its likely results? How can it be avoided?

7. Discuss how social networks facilitate the reproduction of existing inequalities. Pay particular attention to the position of women, lower socioeconomic classes, and minorities in networks. Be sure to discuss the impact of the Internet on these issues.

8. The Internet can be both an advantage and a disadvantage to social relationships. Explain.

9. According to the text, "Democracy flourishes when social capital is strong." Do you agree or disagree? Defend your position using sociological evidence cited in the text.

CHAPTER 7

Conformity, Deviance, and Crime

Multiple-Choice Questions

d (page 179)

1. Deviance
   a. is nonconformity to a given norm or norms accepted by a significant number of people in a society.
   b. can change from time to time.
   c. can be different in different cultures.
   d. All of the above
   e. None of the above

c (pages 178–179)

2. What sociological question is most important to keep in mind when considering deviance?
   a. Who are the deviants and who are the conformists?
   b. Why is the deviant so strange?
   c. Whose rules are being broken?
   d. Why am I not a deviant?
   e. How can we eliminate deviance?

d (page 179)

3. Hackers
   a. are portrayed in the news media as deviants.
   b. have their own ethics.
   c. are participants in a deviant subculture.
   d. All of the above
   e. None of the above

a (page 180)

4. What do sociologists call a group such as the Heaven's Gate cult, which existed by following some social norms but had many of its own that were considered strange by most people?
   a. deviant subculture
   b. deviating normative group
   c. aggregate
   d. social control
   e. sanction

d (page 180)   5. Émile Durkheim's view of deviance is that
    a. in defining what is deviant, we also become aware of what is *not* deviant.
    b. in defining what is deviant, we became aware of the standards we *share* as members of society.
    c. we shouldn't try to totally eliminate deviance, but just keep it under control.
    d. All of the above
    e. None of the above

a (page 180)   6. Kai Erikson built on Émile Durkheim's concept of deviance, concluding that
    a. a society needs a certain quota of deviance in order to function and maintain itself.
    b. the role of police, courts, and psychiatrists is to eliminate deviance and thereby improve society.
    c. the Puritans "defined deviance down," resulting in many of the social problems we face today.
    d. All of the above
    e. None of the above

d (page 181)   7. Individuals become increasingly committed to social norms over time as a result of interactions with others who obey the law. This process is an example of
    a. deviance.
    b. a deviant subculture.
    c. functionalism.
    d. social control theory.
    e. ethnomethodology.

b (page 181)   8. Any reaction from others to the behavior of an individual meant to ensure that individual complies with a given norm is called a
    a. reward.
    b. sanction.
    c. response cry.
    d. punishment.
    e. slap on the wrist.

b (page 181)   9. Sanctions applied by a specific organization or agency, such as a judge, are
    a. informal.
    b. formal.
    c. positive.
    d. negative.
    e. deviant.

a (page 181)

10. Less organized, more spontaneous reactions to nonconformity are called _____ sanctions.
    a. informal
    b. formal
    c. positive
    d. negative
    e. deviant

e (page 181)

11. Formal sanctions defined by governments as principles their citizens must follow are called
    a. prisons.
    b. crimes.
    c. positive reinforcement.
    d. negative reinforcement.
    e. laws.

c (page 184)

12. Early attempts to explain deviant behavior in individuals assumed that crime was committed mostly by people with certain physical traits. This view was called
    a. psychological determinism.
    b. sociological determinism.
    c. biological determinism.
    d. geological determinism.
    e. anthropological determinism.

a (page 184)

13. Withdrawn, emotionless characters who delight in violence for its own sake are known as
    a. psychopaths.
    b. endomorphs.
    c. ectomorphs.
    d. megalomaniacs.
    e. professors.

d (page 185)

14. Which theory sees the source of deviance in the individual?
    a. biological
    b. psychological
    c. sociological
    d. *a* and *b* only
    e. *b* and *c* only

a (page 185)   15. Biological and psychological theories of crime use a
                        positivist approach. This means
                        a. they believe in empirical research as the source of
                            understanding crime and forming policies to deal
                            with it.
                        b. they look for the beneficial effects of criminal
                            behavior.
                        c. they believe positive thinking can solve crime.
                        d. All of the above
                        e. *b* and *c* only

b (page 185)   16. An important emphasis of sociological analysis of
                        deviance is
                        a. that only psychologically disturbed individuals commit
                            deviant acts.
                        b. the interconnection between conformity and deviance
                            in different social contexts.
                        c. that deviance is most likely genetically inherited.
                        d. All of the above
                        e. None of the above

d (page 187)   17. Edwin Sutherland's idea that in a society with a variety of
                        subcultures, some social environments tend to encourage
                        illegal activities is known as
                        a. labeling.
                        b. social deviance.
                        c. nonconformity.
                        d. differential association.
                        e. environmental deviance.

c (pages 187–188)   18. In Edwin Sutherland's theory of deviance, members of a
                        peer group might learn to be delinquent through associating
                        with carriers of
                        a. positive sanctions.
                        b. negative sanctions.
                        c. criminal norms.
                        d. anomie.
                        e. HIV.

b (page 186)

19. Anomie
    a. is a concept first introduced by Robert Merton.
    b. exists when there are no clear standards or norms to guide behavior.
    c. has the ironic effect of reducing suicide rates, according to Émile Durkheim.
    d. All of the above
    e. None of the above

d (page 186)

20. Who adapted the concept of anomie to refer to the strain people experience when norms conflict with the social structural reality they are faced with?
    a. Émile Durkheim
    b. Karl Marx
    c. Max Weber
    d. Robert Merton
    e. Anthony Giddens

a (page 186)

21. In Robert Merton's theory of crime and deviance, _____ accept the values and goals held by the society and the conventional ways of trying to realize those goals.
    a. conformists
    b. innovators
    c. ritualists
    d. retreatists
    e. rebels

b (page 186)

22. Which type reacts to structural strain by accepting socially approved values but using illegitimate means of achieving those ends, according to Robert Merton?
    a. Conformists
    b. Innovators
    c. Ritualists
    d. Retreatists
    e. Rebels

e (page 186)

23. People who reject both the existing values and the means of achieving them, but work to substitute new ones and reconstruct the social system would be what type, according to Robert Merton?
    a. Conformists
    b. Innovators
    c. Ritualists
    d. Retreatists
    e. Rebels

c (page 186)

24. According to Merton, deviance is a byproduct of
   a. certain physical characteristics of the individual.
   b. certain psychological traits of the individual.
   c. the contrast between aspirations and economic inequalities.
   d. All of the above
   e. None of the above

a (page 187)

25. Who used the concept of "delinquent subculture" to refer to groups like gangs who reject middle class norms and celebrate deviance?
   a. Cohen
   b. Merton
   c. Lemert
   d. Hirschi
   e. Brando

b (page 188)

26. _____ theory focuses on the process by which representatives of the power structure in society define who is deviant.
   a. Differential association
   b. Labeling
   c. Structural strain
   d. Anomie
   e. Rational choice

a (page 187)

27. What would be a valid criticism of functionalists like Merton, Cohen, and Cloward and Ohlin?
   a. They assume that middle class values are held by all members of society.
   b. They pay too much attention to white collar crime.
   c. They "blame the victim" in assuming that biological characteristics cause deviance.
   d. All of the above
   e. None of the above

b (page 187)

28. Which theoretical approach sees deviance as socially constructed?
   a. functionalism
   b. interactionism
   c. the new criminology
   d. All of the above
   e. None of the above

c (page 188)

29. In Edwin Lemert's version of labeling theory, the initial violation of social norms is called
   a. anomie.
   b. structural strain.
   c. primary deviation.
   d. secondary deviation.
   e. initiation.

d (page 188)

30. According to Edwin Lemert, when an person accepts a label and sees himself as deviant, he engages in
   a. anomie.
   b. structural strain.
   c. primary deviation.
   d. secondary deviation.
   e. initiation.

c (page 189)

31. Which theoretical approach sees deviance as deliberately chosen behavior, often political in nature?
   a. functionalism
   b. interactionism
   c. the new criminology
   d. All of the above
   e. None of the above

a (page 189)

32. Theorists of the new criminology view laws as
   a. means by which the elite maintain their positions of power in society.
   b. means by which the masses can maintain majority rule.
   c. neutral.
   d. *b* and *c*
   e. None of the above

e (pages 189)

33. Where would you find Marxist influences?
   a. functionalism
   b. the new criminology
   c. New Left Realism
   d. *a* and *b* only
   e. *b* and *c* only

e (page 190)   34. Car alarms are examples of
                        a. anomie.
                        b. labeling.
                        c. deviance.
                        d. New Left Realism.
                        e. target hardening.

e (page 190)   35. The _____ theory of crime argues that any sign of
                        social disorder in a community encourages more serious
                        crime to flourish.
                        a. differential association
                        b. structural strain
                        c. labeling
                        d. "broken legs"
                        e. "broken windows"

a (page 192)   36. Early sociological theories assumed and tried to
                        explain why
                        a. crime was more prevalent among the lower classes.
                        b. crime was more prevalent among the middle
                            classes.
                        c. crime was more prevalent among the upper classes.
                        d. the relationship between class and crime is class and
                            crime specific (i.e., people in different classes are
                            likely to commit different crimes).
                        e. None of the above; there is no relationship between
                            class and crime.

d (pages 192–195)   37. Many sociologists today argue that
                        a. crime is more prevalent among the lower classes.
                        b. crime is more prevalent among the middle
                            classes.
                        c. crime is more prevalent among the upper classes.
                        d. the relationship between class and crime is class and
                            crime specific (i.e., people in different classes are
                            likely to commit different crimes).
                        e. None of the above; there is no relationship between
                            class and crime.

c (pages 191–192)

38. William Chambliss's study, "The Saints and the Roughnecks," shows the connection between _____ factors like the social class structure and _____ issues like labeling.
    a. rational; irrational
    b. emotional; rational
    c. macrosociological; microsociological
    d. microsociological; macrosociological
    e. moral; immoral

b (page 192)

39. Which is probably the most widely used sociological theory analyzing deviance and crime?
    a. differential association
    b. labeling
    c. structural strain
    d. anomie
    e. rational choice analysis

a (page 192)

40. The National Crime Victimization Survey has found that
    a. crime rates are actually higher than those reported by official agencies.
    b. crime rates are actually lower than those reported by official agencies.
    c. crime rates are about the same as those reported by official agencies, confirming the accuracy of those reports.
    d. All of the above—it depends on the type of crime.
    e. None of the above; the survey has nothing to do with actual crime rates.

d (page 192)

41. Who are the most common *victims* of murder and other violent crimes?
    a. older, white, middle class, suburban females
    b. older, white, wealthy, rural males
    c. young, Hispanic, poor, urban females
    d. young, African-American, urban males
    e. middle-aged, Native American, upper middle class, rural males

c (pages 192–194)

42. Rank the following locations in terms of violent crime rates, from highest to lowest:
    a. smaller towns, cities, suburbs.
    b. cities, smaller towns, suburbs.
    c. cities, suburbs, smaller towns.
    d. suburbs, cities, smaller towns.
    e. suburbs, smaller towns, cities.

d (page 194)   43. What factor contributed to the decline of crime rates in the
                        1990s?
                        a.   aggressive law enforcement
                        b.   decline in the crack cocaine epidemic in urban areas
                        c.   the economic boom of the 1990s
                        d.   All of the above
                        e.   None of the above; crime rates have actually risen.

d (pages 194–195)   44. What is the most likely explanation for why violent crime
                        is so prevalent in the United States, compared to other
                        Western societies?
                        a.   the widespread availability of firearms
                        b.   the frontier tradition
                        c.   violent subcultures in the inner cities
                        d.   All of the above
                        e.   None of the above

e (page 196)   45. Otto Pollack's contention that women are naturally more
                        deceitful and skilled at covering up their crimes than men
                        was based on
                        a.   empirical data from the 1950s.
                        b.   empirical data from the 1980s.
                        c.   case studies.
                        d.   sociobiology.
                        e.   groundless stereotypes.

b (page 196)   46. If a female lawbreaker avoids punishment or prosecution
                        by convincing authorities she is impulsive and in need of
                        protection, she has invoked the
                        a.   chivalry thesis.
                        b.   gender contract.
                        c.   Pollack approach.
                        d.   "nice girl" argument.
                        e.   None of the above

a (page 197)   47. Brownmiller argued that rape
                        a.   reinforces male social dominance by keeping all
                             women in fear.
                        b.   is a crime in which the sexual act is the goal and
                             purpose.
                        c.   occurs much less often than is statistically reported.
                        d.   All of the above
                        e.   None of the above

b (page 199)

48. Crime carried out by more affluent members of society is called
   a. organized crime.
   b. white collar crime.
   c. criminal networks.
   d. necktie crime.
   e. None of the above; such crime is negligible and has no term applied to it.

a (page 201)

49. Forms of activity that have some of the characteristics of legitimate business but are illegal are called
   a. organized crime.
   b. white collar crime.
   c. criminal networks.
   d. necktie crime.
   e. None of the above; such crime is negligible and has no term applied to it.

e (page 203)

50. Which country puts the highest number of people per capita in prison?
   a. Russia
   b. China
   c. Cuba
   d. Italy
   e. United States

b (page 201)

51. What became a central feature of the global economy at "the end of the millennium," according Manuel Castells?
   a. a greater sense of global justice
   b. organized crime
   c. declining numbers of countries that are "low risk" for criminal behavior
   d. All of the above
   e. None of the above

c (page 207)

52. Ericson and Haggerty conclude that police have become primarily _____ , engaged in _____ .
   a. deviants; committing rather than preventing crime
   b. corrections officers; herding criminals to prison
   c. knowledge workers; mapping and predicting risk within the population
   d. safety patrols; guarding the health and welfare of citizens
   e. None of the above

d (page 205)   53. Why have governments been unable to stop the flow of
                    illicit drugs, in spite of spending billions of dollars to do
                    so?
                    a.   The profit potential for drug dealers is so great that
                         many are willing to take the risks.
                    b.   Drug traffickers can take advantage of the technologies
                         of globalization.
                    c.   Drug traffickers can take advantage of the extensive
                         globalized trade networks.
                    d.   All of the above
                    e.   None of the above

b (page 205)   54. Sociological studies show that prisons
                    a.   are effective at deterring crime.
                    b.   are more likely to create hardened criminals than
                         rehabilitated citizens.
                    c.   are actually attractive and pleasant places to live.
                    d.   All of the above
                    e.   None of the above

c (page 205)   55. Sociological research and theory suggest that
                    a.   the problem of crime and deviance could easily be
                         solved by building more prisons and increasing
                         incarceration rates.
                    b.   deviance is primarily an inborn character and could be
                         eliminated by genetic engineering.
                    c.   crime and deviance are rooted in the structure of
                         society, including poverty, urban conditions, and the
                         crises faced by many young men.
                    d.   high crime rates are the price we pay for encouraging
                         freedom and nonconformity.
                    e.   None of the above; sociological research on crime and
                         deviance is inconclusive.

True/False Questions

T (page 178)   1. Even "deviant" groups have their own norms to which
                   members are expected to conform.

T (page 178)   2. Most people at some point engage in behavior that could be
                   considered deviant.

F (page 181)   3. The term sanctions refers only to responses meant to punish nonconformity.

F (page 184)   4. Evidence supporting the biological view of the causes of deviance has shown a direct genetic link between physical traits and violent behavior.

T (page 184)   5. The character traits defined as "psychopathic" might also be held by someone who is considered a hero, such as a successful spy.

F (page 188)   6. Labeling theory begins from the assumption that all deviant acts are intrinsically criminal.

T (pages 188–189)   7. The context in which behavior occurs often makes the difference in whether it is considered deviant or criminal.

T (page 194)   8. Since 1991, rates of violent crime have decreased significantly in the United States.

F (pages 199–200)   9. The amount of money involved in crimes against property (robberies, burglaries, larceny, forgeries, and car thefts) is forty times greater than the amount involved in white collar crimes.

F (page 200)   10. White collar crime is essentially nonviolent, since it does not physically harm or kill anyone.

Essay Questions

1. How is it possible that a person can be both a conformist and a deviant? Explain, using examples and sociological concepts and theories.

2. What is a hacker? Do you consider hackers to be deviants? Justify your evaluation using sociological concepts and theory.

3. What distinguishes sociological from biological or psychological theories of deviance?

4. Discuss the interconnections between conformity and deviance in sociological theories.

5. What causes crime, according to control theory? Be sure to define and discuss the four types of social control bonds in Hirschi's analysis.

6. What is the "chivalry thesis" and how is it used to explain the gender discrepancy in crime rates? Is this an adequate explanation for the statistical reality? If so, show why it is superior to other theories. If not, discuss which theory is more compelling, and why.

7. In what ways are crimes against women comparable to crimes against gay men and lesbians? Explain.

8. Why is a drug like ecstasy seen as a danger to society, while one like Prozac is seen to have great benefits? Focus on the ways that deviance is socially defined.

9. In what ways do theories about the causes of crime affect social policies? Choose three theories, and describe which policies might be followed by their adherents.

CHAPTER 8

Stratification, Class, and Inequality

Multiple-Choice Questions

c (page 216)

1. When sociologists study the existence of structured inequalities in a society, they refer to that structure as
   a. social inequity.
   b. social iniquity.
   c. social stratification.
   d. strategic sociality.
   e. socialism.

d (page 216)

2. Social stratification
   a. is built into the social system.
   b. is based on class, status, and power.
   c. can be based on property, gender, age, religious affiliation, and other statuses.
   d. All of the above
   e. None of the above

b (pages 216–217)

3. Which of the following is true of *all* systems of social stratification?
   a. If a person no longer identifies with the other members of his or her category, he or she is no longer classified at that level.
   b. A person's life chances are significantly influenced by his or her position.
   c. Ranks tend to fluctuate rapidly and significantly over time.
   d. All of the above
   e. None of the above

a (page 217)

4. _____ is a stratification system in which certain people are owned as property and more or less deprived of all rights by law.
   a. Slavery
   b. Caste
   c. Estates
   d. All of the above
   e. None of the above

b (page 217)

5. In a _____ system, a person's social status is set at birth and is unchangeable.
   a. slavery
   b. caste
   c. class
   d. communist
   e. capitalist

b (page 218)

6. Forbidding marriage or sex outside one's assigned group is used to maintain a _____ system.
   a. slavery
   b. caste
   c. class
   d. communist
   e. capitalist

a (page 218)

7. In which country was caste based on broad occupational groupings?
   a. India
   b. United States
   c. South Africa
   d. Russia
   e. Saudi Arabia

e (pages 218–219)

8. In the twentieth century, which country had a caste system based on race?
   a. India
   b. United States
   c. South Africa
   d. *a* and *b* only
   e. *b* and *c* only

b (page 219)

9. The term "class" is most often used to analyze stratification in _____ societies.
   a. hunting and gathering
   b. industrialized
   c. feudal
   d. caste
   e. all

d (page 219)

10. What do sociologists call a large group of people who occupy a similar economic position in society?
    a. slaves
    b. caste
    c. estate
    d. class
    e. peons

a (page 219)

11. Max Weber used the concept of _____ to analyze the meaning of social class.
    a. life chances
    b. life course
    c. caste
    d. reincarnation
    e. relations of production

e (pages 219–220)

12. Which of the following characteristics distinguish class systems from slavery and caste systems?
    a. All the other systems have fluid boundaries.
    b. People are born into a class and stay there for life; there is more social mobility in the other systems.
    c. Unlike the others, class is based on personal relationships.
    d. All of the above
    e. None of the above

a (pages 219–220)

13. Which of the following statements about class systems is NOT accurate?
    a. The boundaries between classes are very clear-cut.
    b. Class systems are fluid.
    c. Class positions are in some part achieved.
    d. Class is economically based.
    e. Class systems are impersonal.

b (page 220)

14. According to the Kuznets curve, inequality in capitalist societies
    a. decreases at first, stabilizes, then decreases again.
    b. increases at first, declines, then stabilizes at a relatively low level.
    c. decreases at first, increases rapidly, then stabilizes at a relatively high level.
    d. increases at first, stabilizes at a high level, then declines gradually.
    e. starts out stable for a long time, then gradually increases to a high level.

b (page 222)

15. The money a person gets from a wage or salary or from investments is _____; the assets an individual owns are _____.
    a. wealth; property
    b. income; wealth
    c. wealth; income
    d. income; income
    e. property; property

a (page 221)

16. During the twentieth century, the real income of blue-collar workers in Western societies has _____ overall, though it has _____ in the past twenty years.
    a. increased significantly; dropped
    b. increased significantly; increased only slightly
    c. decreased significantly; increased
    d. decreased slightly; increased significantly
    e. None of the above

d (page 224)

17. What factor accounts for racial disparities in wealth and income?
    a. education
    b. parents' social class
    c. discrimination
    d. All of the above
    e. None of the above

d (page 224)

18. In 1998, the wealthiest one percent of Americans held _____ percent of the nation's total net worth.
    a. 1
    b. 5
    c. 20
    d. 38
    e. 83

a (page 224)

19. Which of the following is a strong predictor of one's occupation, income, and wealth in later life?
    a. educational attainment
    b. religious background of parents
    c. the performance of the stock market
    d. access to technology, like the Internet
    e. All of the above

a (pages 226–229)

20. According to Savage et al's application of Bourdieu's understanding of class distinctions based on cultural tastes and leisure pursuits, which sector of the middle class is high in "cultural capital" and low in "economic capital"?
    a. professionals in public service
    b. managers and bureaucrats
    c. postmoderns
    d. bobos
    e. hobos

b (page 228)

21. According to the text, the upper class in the United States
    a. is made up of the wealthiest 20 percent of the population.
    b. have a distinctive lifestyle and are politically influential.
    c. does not include "new money" entrepreneurs like Bill Gates.
    d. All of the above
    e. None of the above

b (page 229)

22. Mid-level managers and professionals are in the
    a. lower middle class.
    b. upper middle class.
    c. old middle class.
    d. new middle class.
    e. working class.

d (page 229)

23. Members of the lower middle class
    a. may have relatively high status.
    b. make up about 40 percent of American households.
    c. most likely have a high school diploma.
    d. All of the above
    e. None of the above

e (page 230)

24. People working in blue-collar or pink-collar occupations make up the
    a. lower middle class.
    b. upper middle class.
    c. old middle class.
    d. new middle class.
    e. working class.

d (page 230)

25. What caused the emergence of the "new urban poor" in the last quarter century?
    a. economic globalization, which led to high unemployment among the unskilled sectors of the lower class
    b. racial discrimination in hiring for the remaining low-skill jobs in urban centers
    c. changes in government policies that cut back or eliminated welfare programs
    d. All of the above
    e. None of the above

e (page 232)

26. What was the ratio of Gap CEO Millard Drexler's salary to that of the average worker making Gap clothing in 1999?
    a. 8 to 1
    b. 20 to 1
    c. 458 to 1
    d. 1,458 to 1
    e. 216,250 to 1

b (page 233)

27. What accounts for the "wealth gap" between blacks and whites, according to Oliver and Shapiro?
    a. a culture of poverty among African Americans that discourages achievement
    b. the legacy of slavery and discrimination, which provided little or no opportunity to accumulate wealth
    c. the "disorganized" African American family
    d. All of the above
    e. None of the above; there is no wealth gap.

c (pages 234–235)   28. Social mobility refers to
 a. the migration of people to town from the countryside.
 b. the migration of people from the countryside to town.
 c. the movement of individuals and groups between class positions.
 d. the ability of people in a society to engage in protest movements.
 e. the transportation system of a society.

a (page 236)   29. How far an individual moves up or down the socioeconomic scale in her lifetime is called
 a. intragenerational mobility.
 b. intergenerational mobility.
 c. life course.
 d. life history.
 e. structural mobility.

b (pages 235–236)   30. If a person has a different class position than that of his parents or grandparents he has experienced
 a. intragenerational mobility.
 b. intergenerational mobility.
 c. life course.
 d. life history.
 e. exchange mobility.

c (page 235)   31. Suppose a society had truly equal opportunity, and, in each generation, the more talented people move up in position while the least talented move down. Such a society would have
 a. intragenerational mobility.
 b. intergenerational mobility.
 c. exchange mobility.
 d. life history.
 e. structural mobility.

e (page 235)   32. _____ is social mobility resulting from changes in the number and kinds of occupations in a society.
 a. Intragenerational mobility
 b. Intergenerational mobility
 c. Life course
 d. Life history
 e. Structural mobility

c (page 235)

33. According to _____, technological advance leads to more social mobility.
   a. Marx
   b. Sorokin
   c. the industrialism hypothesis
   d. All of the above
   e. None of the above

c (page 236)

34. Studies by Sorokin in the 1920s, Lipset and Bendix in the 1950s, and Erikson and Goldthorpe in the 1990s
   a. supported the industrialism hypothesis.
   b. slightly modified the industrialism hypothesis, but supported it overall.
   c. found evidence that did not support the industrialism hypothesis.
   d. focused on intragenerational mobility.
   e. resulted in the post-industrial hypothesis.

d (pages 236–237)

35. Studies of social mobility from Peter Blau and Otis Dudley Duncan's in the 1960s to Pierre Bourdieu's in the 1980s have shown that
   a. educational attainment has a great deal to do with ultimate social status.
   b. the family's social status affects the child's educational attainment.
   c. both economic and cultural capital are inherited.
   d. All of the above
   e. None of the above

d (page 237)

36. The term that Pierre Bourdieu uses for the advantages that a "good home" confers, such as a parent's involvement with a child's homework, is
   a. status.
   b. prestige.
   c. life chance.
   d. social capital.
   e. cultural wealth.

b (pages 246–247) 37. In their classic study of social mobility in the United States, Peter Blau and Otis Dudley Duncan found that
a. the rags to riches story was quite common.
b. vertical mobility was common, but usually between occupational positions quite close to one another.
c. surprisingly, educational attainment was not a factor in vertical mobility.
d. there has been little upward mobility.
e. All of the above

b (page 242) 38. The condition in which people do not have adequate resources to maintain their health is called
a. relative poverty.
b. absolute poverty.
c. downward mobility.
d. exchange mobility.
e. the poverty line.

b (page 242) 39. When one is poor compared to the standards of living of most people, she experiences
a. relative poverty.
b. absolute poverty.
c. downward mobility.
d. exchange mobility.
e. upward mobility.

c (pages 242–243) 40. The 1999 poverty rate in the United States was about _____ percent, using a poverty line set at three times the cost of a nutritional diet. A more realistic estimate using a poverty line at six times the food expenditure would give a poverty rate of about _____ percent.
a. 2; 4
b. 4; 2
c. 12; 24
d. 15; 30
e. None of the above; the poverty line is not calculated that way.

d (page 252) 41. The fastest-growing group among the homeless population in the United States is
a. substance abusers.
b. the mentally ill.
c. doctors.
d. families with children.
e. Vietnam veterans.

b (page 254)

42. In Karl Marx's theory, a class is made up of people who have the same relationship to the
    a. forces of nature.
    b. means of production.
    c. means of consumption.
    d. state.
    e. next generation.

e (page 254)

43. Karl Marx called those who own the means of production _____ and those who make their living by selling their own labor power for a wage _____.
    a. meanies; sellers
    b. producers; consumers
    c. merchants; peddlers
    d. working class; capitalists
    e. capitalists; the working class

a (page 254)

44. The source of the capitalist's profit, according to Marx, is _____, taken by exploiting the worker—paying her less than the true value of her work.
    a. surplus value
    b. surplus profit
    c. prestige
    d. the means of production
    e. the forces of nature

d (page 254)

45. Max Weber's concept of _____ is based on the amount of social honor, or _____ individuals or groups are given by others.
    a. class; power
    b. power; class
    c. prestige; status
    d. status; prestige
    e. class; surplus value

e (page 254)

46. Max Weber referred to negatively privileged status groups as
    a. capitalists.
    b. working class.
    c. contradictory class locations.
    d. deviants.
    e. pariah groups.

c (page 255) 47. _____ argued that social stratification is functional, ensuring that the most talented people fill the roles they are best suited for by rewarding them accordingly.
   a. Karl Marx
   b. Max Weber
   c. Kingsley Davis and Wilbert E. Moore
   d. Melvin Tumin
   e. Erik Olin Wright

a (page 256) 48. According to Erik Olin Wright, people who control workers but are in turn controlled by their own employers are in
   a. contradictory class locations.
   b. pariah groups.
   c. the capitalist class.
   d. the working class.
   e. a caste.

c (page 257) 49. Frank Parkin uses the concept of _____ to refer to a process through which a group tries to maintain control over resources and limits access to them by other groups.
   a. contradictory class location
   b. pariah group
   c. social closure
   d. social stratification
   e. caste

d (pages 226–227) 50. How has globalization contributed to the increasing inequality in American society?
   a. Some companies have lowered wages to compete with other companies that use cheaper Third World labor.
   b. Globalization has encouraged immigration to the United States, thus increasing the low wage labor pool and pushing wages down.
   c. Labor unions have been weakened by globalization.
   d. All of the above
   e. None of the above; inequality is *not* increasing in the United States.

True/False Questions

F (page 217)   1. By the end of the nineteenth century, human slavery had been eliminated from the world once and for all.

T (page 219)   2. It is much easier for a person to experience social mobility in a class system than in a caste system.

F (pages 222–224)   3. People from humble backgrounds have as much of a chance at becoming wealthy in the United States as do people from more prosperous backgrounds.

F (page 221)   4. Over the past century, Western societies have virtually eliminated the income inequality that characterized earlier eras.

F (page 236)   5. Seymore Martin Lipset and Reinhard Bendix found that the United States has more upward mobility than other western societies.

T (page 237)   6. Educational attainment and the social class of one's parents are both strong predictors of one's class position.

T (page 254)   7. Max Weber argued that class divisions derive from resources such as people's skills, credentials, and qualifications.

T (page 255)   8. Kingsley Davis and Wilbert E. Moore provided a functionalist explanation of stratification, arguing that it has beneficial consequences to society.

T (page 256)   9. According to Erik Olin Wright's theory of class stratification, the class structure is based on three dimensions of control over economic resources: money capital, physical means of production, and labor power.

F (pages 257–258)   10. Globalization of the economy has contributed to a significant decrease in wealth and income inequality in the United States.

Essay Questions

1. Compare and contrast slavery, caste, and class as systems of stratification. What is the basis of inequality in each? How much social mobility exists in each? How do trends in economic development, specifically technology and globalization, affect each of these systems?

2. What is the difference between *income* and *wealth?* What is the relationship between them? How to they relate to one's class position?

3. Describe changes in the distribution of income and wealth in the United States over the last thirty years. Is there a recognizable trend? Apply one of the stratification theories discussed in the chapter to explain this trend.

4. Discuss the differences in average income and wealth between whites, African Americans, and Latinos. Are the gaps shrinking or getting larger? Why?

5. Using what you have learned about the lower class, construct an imaginary family that might be typical of this class in the United States. Describe their way of life and the prospects for their future.

6. What is the difference between *intergenerational* and *intragenerational* mobility? What factors influence the amount of each? Refer to specific research on the topic, including cross-national studies and comparisons of mobility for women and men.

7. Explain how you would support a family of four on the 1999 poverty line income of $16,900 per year.

8. Discuss the trend known as "the feminization of poverty." How has this affected the number and percentage of children living in poverty in the United States?

9. Discuss the existence of the homeless in American society. What is their significance? How do sociologists attempt to understand this phenomenon? Cite specific studies.

10. Discuss the process and forms of social exclusion that affect social stratification. Explain the significance of this statement from the text: "In considering the phenomenon of social exclusion we must once again be conscious of the interaction between human agency and responsibility on the one hand, and the role of social forces in shaping people's circumstances on the other hand."

CHAPTER 9
Global Inequality

Multiple-Choice Questions

a (page 261)

1. In 2000, the richest person in the world was
    a. Bill Gates.
    b. Paul Allen.
    c. Wirat Tasago.
    d. Li Ka-shing.
    e. Anthony Giddens.

d (page 262)

2. Of the 20 richest people in the world in the year 2000, how many were Americans?
    a. 1
    b. 2
    c. 5
    d. 10
    e. 20

c (page 262)

3. A country's annual output of goods and services per person is its
    a. global inequality.
    b. global per-person output (GPO).
    c. per person gross domestic product (GDP).
    d. per capita product (PCP).
    e. gross output over duties (GOOD).

c (page 263)

4. A country has a per person GDP of $10,000. This country is _____ income, according to the World Bank.
    a. low-
    b. middle-
    c. high-
    d. upper-middle
    e. lower-middle

d (page 263)

5. Which of the following is a high-income country?
   a. United States
   b. Japan
   c. Singapore
   d. All of the above
   e. None of the above

e (page 266)

6. Because China has hundreds of millions of people living in poverty it is classified as a _____ country by the World Bank.
   a. low income
   b. extremely poor
   c. Third World
   d. All of the above
   e. None of the above; the World Bank classifies countries based on average income, not numbers of poor people.

b (page 266)

7. The _____ countries comprised 45 percent of the world's population but produced 18 percent of the wealth in 1999.
   a. low-income
   b. middle-income
   c. high-income
   d. socialist
   e. fascist

d (page 266)

8. The main economic activity in most low-income countries is
   a. high technology.
   b. oil production.
   c. mining.
   d. agriculture.
   e. manufacturing.

a (page 267)

9. Global inequality is
   a. growing.
   b. lessening.
   c. staying the same.
   d. varying from year to year, with no distinct trend.
   e. unmeasurable.

c (page 268)

10. What proportion of the world's population lives in poverty?
    a. 1 percent
    b. one tenth
    c. one fourth
    d. about half
    e. None of the above; the concept is relative and therefore meaningless.

e (page 272)

11. Most famine and hunger in the world today are the outcome of
    a. overpopulation.
    b. organic farming.
    c. a global shortage of food.
    d. a global glut of food.
    e. a combination of natural and social forces.

e (page 272)

12. As world hunger has grown, global food production
    a. has declined, exacerbating the hunger problem.
    b. has failed to keep up with population growth.
    c. began to fall behind population growth in the 1990s.
    d. was already declining, and has declined even more rapidly as hunger has increased.
    e. has actually continued to increase more rapidly than population growth.

b (page 272)

13. Education and literacy clearly contribute to economic development and individual social mobility. Which countries have the highest percentage of their youth attending secondary school?
    a. low-income, because they see this as an important strategy for development
    b. high-income
    c. middle-income, because they have enough surplus product and see the need for education
    d. All of the above have about equal percentages attending secondary school.
    e. Attendance at secondary school has nothing to do with development.

d (page 273)

14. Rapid economic growth in East Asia in the 1980s and 1990s was accompanied by
    a. violent suppression of labor rights.
    b. development of an increasingly female and immigrant, exploited labor force.
    c. environmental degradation.
    d. All of the above
    e. None of the above

b (page 273)

15. Most of the NIEs in East Asia today are
    a. low-income countries.
    b. middle-income countries.
    c. high-income countries.
    d. just starting to develop.
    e. not yet ready for "take-off."

b (page 273)

16. The rapidly growing economies of the world are known as
    a. Rapidly Growing Economies (RGEs).
    b. Newly Industrializing Economies (NIEs).
    c. Rapidly Industrializing Regions (RIRs).
    d. Rapidly Industrializing Countries (RICs).
    e. Blast-off Industrializing Countries (BICs).

d (page 273)

17. Which region experienced such rapid economic growth between the 1960s and 1980s that most of its NIEs moved from the ranks of the poor to the middle-income category?
    a. East Africa
    b. Northern Europe
    c. Central America
    d. East Asia
    e. South Asia

d (page 273)

18. Rapid economic development in East Asia has clearly had its benefits. Which of the following was among the costs?
    a. violent repression of labor and civil rights
    b. exploitation of women and immigrants
    c. widespread environmental degradation
    d. All of the above
    e. None of the above was a significant factor in East Asia.

a (page 273)

19. Which of the following was among the reasons East Asia experienced rapid economic growth from the mid-1970s to the mid-1990s?
    a. Countries like Taiwan, South Korea, and Hong Kong actually benefited in key ways from colonialism.
    b. The countries were growing while the rest of the world was experiencing economic crisis.
    c. These countries received important economic aid from the Soviet Union during the Cold War.
    d. All of the above
    e. None of the above; these countries did not experience economic development during that period.

d (page 275)

20. In the late 1990s, economic development in the East Asian NIEs
    a. continued at a rapid pace.
    b. accelerated rapidly to the fastest pace in world history.
    c. slowed somewhat, but continued at an unprecedented pace.
    d. came to an abrupt halt because of corruption, poor investments, and world economic conditions.
    e. came to a sudden halt because of government intervention in the economy.

a (page 278)

21. The most influential theories of global inequality among Western economists and sociologists in the 1960s were
    a. market-oriented theories.
    b. modernization theories.
    c. dependency theories.
    d. world systems theories.
    e. state-centered theories.

d (page 279)

22. Which stage immediately follows "take-off," according to Rostow's modernization theory?
    a. traditional stage
    b. landing
    c. mid-flight cruising altitude
    d. drive to technological maturity
    e. mass consumption

c (page 279)

23. _____, a view now commonly held by Western economists, is based on _____ theory, which promoted free markets and non-interference by governments in the economy.
    a. Marxism; dependency
    b. Liberalism; state-centered development
    c. Neo-liberalism; modernization
    d. Neo-Marxism; world systems
    e. Conservatism; arcane

b (page 280)

24. What was the original cause of "misdevelopment" in the low-income countries, according to dependency theory?
    a. their backward, fatalistic value systems
    b. colonialism
    c. their peripheral geographical locations
    d. All of the above
    e. None of the above

a (page 281)

25. According to world-systems theory, the global economic system must be approached as a single _____ unit, not as a collection of independent, individual countries.
    a. capitalist
    b. socialist
    c. communist
    d. fascist
    e. None of the above

a (page 281)

26. Which countries are the most advanced industrial societies, collecting the greatest share of the economic pie, according to world-systems theory?
    a. core
    b. peripheral
    c. semi-peripheral
    d. semi-core
    e. hemisperipheral

b (page 281)

27. Natural resources flow from the _____ to the _____, according to world-systems theory.
    a. core; periphery
    b. periphery; core
    c. semi-periphery; periphery
    d. upper class; lower class
    e. north; south

e (page 281)   28. Which countries exploit the natural resources of the
                    periphery, according to world-systems theory?
                    a. core
                    b. semi-core
                    c. semi-peripheral
                    d. *a* and *b*
                    e. *a* and *c*

c (page 281)   29. In _____, networks of labor, production, and
                    consumption of products span the world.
                    a. world wide work
                    b. semi-peripheral chains
                    c. global commodity chains
                    d. dependency theory
                    e. net span theory

d (pages 284–285) 30. Sweatshops are
                    a. illegal.
                    b. often "firetraps."
                    c. reappearing in major U.S. cities.
                    d. All of the above
                    e. None of the above

e (pages 278–284) 31. Which of the following statements is *true?*
                    a. World-systems theory and market-centered theories
                        agree that backward cultures are the source of world
                        poverty.
                    b. Barbie is made in the United States.
                    c. Democratic countries in East Asia like Taiwan and
                        South Korea underwent rapid economic growth
                        because they supported the rights of workers and kept
                        their hands off business.
                    d. All of the above
                    e. None of the above

e (page 286)   32. Which approach points out that successful NIEs such as
                    Singapore, South Korea, and Taiwan have grown largely
                    because of repressive labor laws, government ownership in
                    key industries, and government provision of social welfare
                    services?
                    a. market-oriented theory
                    b. modernization theory
                    c. dependency theory
                    d. world-systems theory
                    e. state-centered theory

a (page 286)   33. Which theory promotes the adoption of Western capitalist
economic systems and values as the road to economic
development?
a.   market-oriented theory
b.   Marxist theory
c.   dependency theory
d.   world-systems theory
e.   state-centered theory

c (page 286)   34. Which theory draws primary attention to the exploitation of
poor countries by rich ones?
a.   market-oriented theory
b.   modernization theory
c.   dependency theory
d.   world-systems theory
e.   state-centered theory

d (page 287)   35. Which theory looks at the whole world economy as an
integrated web of relations, rather than focusing on
individual countries?
a.   market-oriented theory
b.   modernization theory
c.   dependency theory
d.   world-systems theory
e.   state-centered theory

e (page 287)   36. Which theory sees an important role for government
coordination and planning in economic development
for NIEs?
a.   market-oriented theory
b.   modernization theory
c.   dependency theory
d.   world-systems theory
e.   state-centered theory

a (page 288)   37. Using Jeffrey Sachs's categories, as which type of region
would the United States be classified?
a.   technology innovators
b.   technology adaptors
c.   technologically disconnected
d.   technologically discombobulated
e.   None of the above

b (page 288)

38. The _____ are regions of the world that apply technology invented elsewhere in their own production and consumption systems.
    a. technology innovators
    b. technology adaptors
    c. technologically disconnected
    d. technologically discombobulated
    e. None of the above

c (page 288)

39. Using Jeffrey Sachs's categories, as which type of region would tropical sub-Saharan Africa be classified?
    a. technology innovators
    b. technology adaptors
    c. technologically disconnected
    d. technologically discombobulated
    e. None of the above

a (page 288)

40. Based on his research on technology and development, Sachs recommends
    a. that wealthy countries provide more financial and technical aid to poor countries to help them overcome obstacles to their adoption and development of science and technology.
    b. that wealthy nations protect their lead in science and technology against potential competition from poor countries.
    c. that poor countries give up on trying to compete with wealthy countries, and accept their role as providers of cheap labor and raw materials.
    d. All of the above
    e. None of the above

d (pages 288–289)

41. The most optimistic analysts expect
    a. the republics of the former Soviet Union to become high-income countries.
    b. economic growth to spread to areas that have lagged behind, like Latin America and Africa.
    c. the remnants of caste societies to be superceded by class-based systems.
    d. All of the above
    e. None of the above

b (page 276)

42. Regarding child labor,
    a. children in the developing countries are protected by the same laws as those in the United States.
    b. one out of every four children in the developing world work, often in hazardous conditions.
    c. slave-like conditions and bonded labor have been eliminated worldwide, thanks to the United Nations.
    d. All of the above
    e. None of the above

c (page 277)

43. In what way(s) could you personally help reduce the amount of exploitive and dangerous child labor in the world today?
    a. Avoid clothing that is made by unionized labor.
    b. Look for clothing made in Myanmar, a country with strong commitments to human rights.
    c. Buy clothing that is certified "sweatshop free" by a reputable organization, like those with the "Rugmark" label.
    d. All of the above
    e. None of the above

d (page 282)

44. Why do women make up such a large portion of the global workforce?
    a. They are often forced to work by husbands or parents who need the extra income.
    b. They often choose to work to gain economic security and independence.
    c. They can usually find jobs with better working conditions than those for men and children.
    d. *a* and *b*
    e. *b* and *c*

c (page 282)

45. Women's role in the global economy
    a. has been widely studied; perhaps even more than that of men.
    b. has really been so insignificant that it is not worth studying.
    c. has not been completely realized in most of the research literature.
    d. has been recognized only in places where women have played a significant role in social revolution, such as Vietnam.
    e. None of the above

a (page 266)

46. Most of the lowest income countries (per capita GNP $755 or less) are found in
    a. Central Africa.
    b. Central America.
    c. North America.
    d. South America.
    e. Western Europe.

a (pages 270–271)

47. In which region would you find the most hunger?
    a. Central Africa
    b. Central America
    c. North America
    d. South America
    e. Western Europe

c (page 266)

48. Which of the following regions do more of the world's recent technological innovations come from?
    a. Central Africa
    b. Central America
    c. North America
    d. South America
    e. Central Asia

e (page 268)

49. In 1999, the average person in a high-income country made _____ the average income of a person in a low-income country.
    a. twice
    b. three times
    c. 20 times
    d. 42 times
    e. 63 times

True/False Questions

T (page 263)

1. GDP does not give a complete picture of economic activity in a country, since it does not include noncash transactions.

T (page 269)

2. In the poorest regions of the world, such as sub-Saharan Africa, a child is more likely to die before age five than to enter secondary school.

F (pages 269–272)   3. Most malnourished children live in countries that cannot produce enough food to feed their own people.

F (page 272)   4. The higher the literacy and education rate in a country, the higher its population growth rate is likely to be.

T (page 273)   5. Some formerly low-income countries in East Asia have actually moved into the high-income category.

F (page 273)   6. Economic development in regions like East Asia has been accompanied by other social gains: an increase in civil rights, the elimination of economic exploitation, and improved environmental protection.

T (page 278)   7. Economic development is most likely to proceed when governments just "get out of the way," according to market-oriented theories.

F (page 279)   8. Neoliberalism is based on the Marxist rejection of market-oriented theories of development.

F (page 287)   9. Rapid globalization is unlikely to have an impact on you personally, since you already live in a high-income country.

T (page 282)   10. Women are often seen by employers as "ideal" workers because they are thought to be less likely to protest abusive conditions.

Essay Questions

1. Why are populations growing more than twice as fast in low-income countries than in high-income countries?

2. Summarize the differences between high- and low-income countries in terms of health, education and literacy, and energy consumption.

3. Detail the factors that were suggested by sociologists as reasons for the rapid economic growth of NIEs in East Asia during the last half of the twentieth century. How might these factors account for the sudden crisis in these economies in the 1990s?

4. Of the theories of global inequality discussed in the text, which would you see as most ethnocentric? Explain.

5. Compare and contrast market-oriented theory with dependency theory on their positions regarding the role of governments in development.

6. What are the four elements of the world system, according to world system theory? How are these elements interconnected?

7. Trace the global commodity chain involved in the production and sale of the Mattel toy, Barbie.

8. What does state-centered theory add to the debate over the causes of (and solutions to) global inequality? Show how state-centered theory helps to explain growth in several economies in East Asia during the 1980s and early 1990s.

9. What are the likely outcomes of the current trend of rapid globalization? Pay particular attention to the significance of developments in the People's Republic of China. How will these changes likely affect you, personally?

10. How could the wealthy countries help the poor countries overcome the technology gap, according to Jeffrey Sachs? What specific measures would help? Why do you think these steps have not been taken?

11. What can be done about the problem of child labor in developing countries? What specific steps can you take personally to make a difference?

12. Discuss the exploitation of women in factories throughout the world. Why would women take such jobs in the first place?

CHAPTER 10

Gender Inequality

Multiple-Choice Questions

a (page 293)   1. Scholars use the term _____ to refer to biological differences between men and women.
a. sex
b. gender
c. biosex
d. biogender
e. sexuality

b (page 293)   2. Scholars use the term _____ to refer to the psychological, social, and cultural differences between women and men.
a. sex
b. gender
c. biosex
d. biogender
e. sexuality

b (page 294)   3. Sociological critics of *gender socialization* point out that
a. testosterone increases aggression in monkeys; gender is clearly biologically determined.
b. humans are active participants in their socialization, not passive recipients of "gender programming" by "agencies of socialization."
c. agencies of socialization ensure socialization by making sure children receive proper gender socialization.
d. All of the above
e. None of the above

a (page 294)   4. Gender socialization begins
a. at birth.
b. around age two or three years.
c. when the child starts school.
d. at puberty.
e. None of the above; gender is an inborn trait.

c (page 296)

5. In recent years, a growing number of sociologists (like Connell, Butler, Scott and Morgan) have argued that
   a. only gender is socially constructed; sex is clearly biological.
   b. only sex is socially constructed; gender is clearly biological.
   c. both gender and sex are socially constructed.
   d. neither gender or sex are socially constructed.
   e. None of the above; views on these issues have remained essentially the same for a long time.

c (page 297)

6. In her classic study of gender roles in three New Guinea tribes, Margaret Mead found
   a. they all had essentially the same gender roles as those in the United States.
   b. the gender roles in all three were exactly reversed from those in the United States.
   c. gender roles varied significantly from one tribe to the other.
   d. the gender roles varied slightly, but none were essentially different from those in the United States.
   e. None of the above; Mead's results were inconclusive, as there were no gender roles defined in any of the cultures.

e (page 297)

7. Which gender is the dominant and aggressive one among the !Kung of the Kalahari Desert?
   a. the men, because they provide most of the food
   b. the women, especially in their authoritarian approach to child rearing
   c. Both men and women are aggressive, leading to a constant "battle of the sexes."
   d. Men are aggressive in providing most of the food, but women are aggressive when it comes to sex.
   e. None of the above; aggressive behavior is discouraged for both genders in !Kung society.

a (page 298)   8. What is the term used for individuals in some Asian, South
                   Pacific, and North American societies who adopt the
                   gender behavior ascribed by their culture for members of
                   the opposite sex?
                   a. *berdache*
                   b. transvestite
                   c. androgynous
                   d. All of the above
                   e. None of the above; no such behavior is accepted in any
                       known culture.

b (page 297)   9. Variations in gender roles found in the many different
                   societies studied by social scientists demonstrate that
                   a. gender roles are biologically determined.
                   b. gender roles are culturally determined.
                   c. social scientists are biased and can't understand gender
                       roles.
                   d. there is no such thing as gender roles.
                   e. gender roles are essentially the same everywhere, with
                       only minor variations.

a (page 299)   10. Male dominance in a society is called
                   a. patriarchy.
                   b. matriarchy.
                   c. masculinity.
                   d. *berdache*.
                   e. the "Y" factor.

e (page 299)   11. _____ refers to any difference in status, power, and
                   prestige between men and women in groups, collectives,
                   and societies.
                   a. Patriarchy
                   b. Matriarchy
                   c. Masculinity
                   d. *Berdache*
                   e. Gender inequality

c (page 300)   12. Over the last fifty years, women's participation in the paid
                   labor force
                   a. has gone up and down with no clear pattern.
                   b. has dropped steadily.
                   c. has risen steadily.
                   d. dropped for the first twenty-five years, but has risen for
                       the last twenty-five.
                   e. rose for the first twenty-five years, but has dropped for
                       the last twenty-five.

d (page 301)   13. _____ occurs when women are steered into poorly paid jobs with few prospects for career advancement.
a. Patriarchy
b. Matriarchy
c. Masculinization
d. Gender typing
e. Gender filing

d (page 303)   14. Although in the past thirty years the pay gap between men and women has _____, it is true that on average _____.
a. increased slightly; pay rates are essentially equal
b. increased a lot; women make substantially more than men
c. narrowed; women make substantially more than men
d. narrowed; men make substantially more than women
e. None of the above; there has been no change in the pay gap in this period.

c (page 305)   15. _____ is a policy that compares pay rates for different jobs based on a presumably objective assessment of skill, effort, responsibility, and working conditions.
a. Patriarchy
b. Gender typing
c. Comparable worth
d. Comparable work
e. Glass ceiling

e (pages 305–306)   16. An organization with a promotion barrier that prevents a woman's upward mobility is said to have
a. patriarchy.
b. gender typing.
c. comparable worth.
d. comparable work.
e. a glass ceiling.

d (page 306)   17. Men in traditionally female occupations often experience a _____, according to a 1992 study by Christine Williams.
a. patriarchy
b. matriarchy
c. comparable worth problem
d. glass escalator
e. glass ceiling

c (page 307)   18. Unwanted or repeated sexual advances, remarks, or
                        behavior that are offensive to the recipient and cause
                        discomfort or interference with job performance constitute
                        a. patriarchy.
                        b. gender typing.
                        c. sexual harassment.
                        d. a glass escalator.
                        e. a glass ceiling.

b (page 307)   19. Since men usually have more _____ than women,
                        women are more often the victims of sexual harassment.
                        a. sex drive
                        b. power
                        c. intelligence
                        d. All of the above
                        e. None of the above

a (page 307)   20. Which type of sexual harassment involves the demand for
                        sexual favors as a condition of the job or in return for work-
                        related benefits?
                        a. *quid pro quo*
                        b. *quid pro bono*
                        c. hostile work environment
                        d. All of the above
                        e. None of the above

c (page 310)   21. When it comes to work in the home, women do most of the
                        _____ while men do most of the _____.
                        a. housework; child care
                        b. child care; housework
                        c. daily chores; occasional tasks
                        d. occasional tasks; daily chores
                        e. dusting; sweeping

d (pages 309–310)   22. Which of the following has been offered as a sociological
explanation for the gap between women's and men's work
in the home?
  a.   Women do most of the housework in exchange for
       economic support from men.
  b.   Men do the jobs that give them the most control over
       when to do them.
  c.   When the daily tasks of work in the home are divided
       along the traditional gender lines (woman-as-server,
       man-as-provider), men and women "do gender" and
       reproduce the gender roles they were socialized with.
  d.   All of the above
  e.   None of the above

d (page 310)   23. In schools, boys and girls are treated unequally
  a.   in stories and books.
  b.   in the frequency of interaction with teachers.
  c.   in the content of their interaction with teachers.
  d.   All of the above
  e.   None of the above

a (page 312)   24. As a result of differential treatment in schools, girls are
socialized to be
  a.   quiet.
  b.   inquisitive.
  c.   active problem solvers.
  d.   All of the above
  e.   None of the above

a (page 318)   25. According to the functionalist sociologist Talcott Parsons,
the family is most efficient when it operates with a clear
sexual division of labor, with the females performing the
_____ role and males performing the _____ role.
  a.   expressive; instrumental
  b.   instrumental; expressive
  c.   gender; sex
  d.   sex; gender
  e.   None of the above; Parsons did not believe in a sexual
       division of labor.

c (page 319)

26. Feminists criticize the *maternal deprivation thesis*, which asserts that children will be _____ if not raised by their own mother or a female mother-substitute.
    a. normal
    b. socialized
    c. inadequately socialized
    d. maternal
    e. None of the above

b (page 322)

27. Which of the following is a broad trend in society that might affect the individual life of a person like Andrea, the example given in the "Gender Inequality" chapter of the textbook?
    a. the decline in women's participation in the labor market
    b. the increase in women's participation in the labor market, but in limited sectors
    c. the increasing strength of the institution of marriage, particularly in poor inner city neighborhoods
    d. All of the above
    e. None of the above

c (page 322)

28. What kind of job is most likely open to a woman like Andrea, the young African-American single mother used as an example in the "Gender Inequality" chapter of the textbook?
    a. highly skilled, well-paid professional
    b. skilled blue collar at a comfortable wage
    c. low wage service work with non-standard working hours
    d. All of the above; opportunities are no different for her than for anyone else.
    e. None of the above; there are simply no jobs available to someone like Andrea.

d (page 323)

29. In the "Gender Inequality" chapter of the textbook, what is the explanation for why a woman like Andrea is more likely to be a single mother?
    a. The increase in women's participation in the labor force has given women more power in the family.
    b. The increase in women's participation in the labor force has given women more independence from men, including the fathers of their children.
    c. Economic restructuring in the 1980s caused a decline in better paid jobs for African-American men, making it more difficult for them to help support a family with children.
    d. All of the above
    e. None of the above

c (page 322)

30. As emphasized in the "Gender Inequality" chapter of the textbook, Andrea's life and the difficulties she faces can be analyzed by
    a. looking at the biological basis of gender inequality.
    b. speculating how her life would be different if she did not have children.
    c. thinking about the inequalities in her life in terms of gender, race, and class.
    d. measuring how much she conforms to society's norms and values.
    e. All of the above

a (page 319)

31. Which of the following assumptions is shared by all of the schools of feminist thought?
    a. that women have an unequal position in society
    b. a rejection of the idea that gender has an influence on social life
    c. a belief that the roots of gender inequality are in biology
    d. All of the above
    e. None of the above

a (page 319)

32. Which perspective explains gender inequalities in terms of social and cultural attitudes, and argues for solutions that involve working in the existing system toward gradual reform?
    a. liberal feminism
    b. radical feminism
    c. black feminism
    d. Parsonian functionalism
    e. Marxism

d (page 320) 33. _____ is the systematic domination of females by males.
a. Gender
b. Sex
c. Matriarchy
d. Patriarchy
e. Malefaction

b (page 320) 34. Which perspective argues that men are responsible for and benefit from the exploitation of women, and advocates abolition of the family and the power relations that characterize it?
a. liberal feminism
b. radical feminism
c. black feminism
d. Parsonian functionalism
e. Marxism

c (page 321) 35. Which perspective focuses on the interaction of race, class, and gender in the disadvantages faced by women?
a. liberal feminism
b. radical feminism
c. black feminism
d. Parsonian functionalism
e. Marxism

c (page 303) 36. In 1994, women earned _____ of what men earned, on average, for working full time.
a. 50 percent
b. 65 percent
c. 76 percent
d. 98 percent
e. 100 percent

b (page 303) 37. _____ means that women and men are concentrated in different occupations.
a. Socialist construction of work
b. Sex segregation
c. Sex integration
d. Gender concentration
e. Radical feminism

a (page 302)

38. In 1998, women held over 95 percent of the jobs in which of the following occupations?
    a. secretary
    b. college professor
    c. taxi driver
    d. lawyer
    e. None of the above

d (page 303)

39. Which of the following occupations were over 80 percent male in 1989?
    a. doctor
    b. lawyer
    c. truck driver
    d. All of the above
    e. None of the above

b (page 303)

40. Sex segregation results in _____ for _____.
    a. higher pay; both men and women in predominantly female jobs
    b. lower pay; both men and women in predominantly female jobs
    c. higher pay; men in female jobs than men in male jobs
    d. the same pay; women in female jobs as men in male jobs
    e. the same pay; women in male jobs as men in female jobs

c (page 303)

41. Despite the Pay Equity Act of 1963, the gender gap in pay has not been eliminated because of
    a. liberal feminism.
    b. radical feminism.
    c. sex segregation.
    d. All of the above
    e. None of the above

b (page 305)

42. _____ is a policy that would pay employees based on the worth of their work rather than the personal characteristics of the majority of workers in that job.
    a. Radical feminism
    b. Comparable worth
    c. Comparable work
    d. Sex segregation
    e. Gender typing

a (page 304)

43. An economic theory that suggests people who invest more in their schooling, on-the-job training, and work experience get paid more is known as the
    a. human capital theory.
    b. human labor theory.
    c. human investment theory.
    d. gender typing theory.
    e. stereotyping theory.

d (page 304)

44. According to the human capital theory, women earn less than men on average because
    a. women have not chosen to "invest" as much in their schooling and job skills.
    b. women choose occupations that are easier to move in and out of.
    c. employers are less likely to "invest" in their female employees because they believe the women will have more interruptions in their careers, e.g., for child rearing.
    d. All of the above
    e. None of the above

d (page 305)

45. Which of the following is a criticism of the human capital theory made by feminist sociologists?
    a. Due to childhood socialization in traditional gender roles, women are not as free to choose their occupations as the theory suggests.
    b. Women are prevented from entering certain occupations due to discrimination by "gatekeepers" on the job.
    c. The difference in power between men and women in society limits women from redefining their occupations as "skilled."
    d. All of the above
    e. None of the above

d (page 326)

46. Where can one find the women's movement?
    a. United States
    b. China
    c. Russia
    d. All of the above
    e. None of the above

c (page 326)

47. What agency has helped develop ties among women's movements in countries around the world?
    a. the men's movement
    b. the International Roundtable of Global Corporations (IRGC)
    c. the United Nations Conference on Women
    d. All of the above
    e. None of the above; no such ties currently exist.

b (page 327)

48. What is the goal of the United Nations Conference on Women?
    a. to promote the traditional role of women in bearing children, raising them, and ensuring the domestic tranquillity of the home
    b. to ensure women's equal access to economic resources including land, credit, science and technology, vocational training, information, communication, and markets
    c. to ensure that no country interferes with the gender role definitions of another
    d. All of the above
    e. None of the above

d (page 327)

49. Which of the following issues is addressed in the Platform for Action agreed to at the 1995 United Nations women's conference in Beijing?
    a. the burden of poverty on women
    b. violence against women
    c. inequality between men and women in power and decision-making
    d. All of the above
    e. None of the above

c (pages 299–312)

50. Overall, sociologists conclude that
    a. biology is destiny—the gender roles of men and women are fixed by their physical differences.
    b. culture plays a minor role in defining gender roles, but biology is the main influence.
    c. biology creates physical differences between women and men, but culture plays the central role in defining specific gender roles.
    d. biology plays no role in the differences between men and women—culture is the only force determining gender differences.
    e. None of the above; sociologists simply can't make up their minds on this issue.

True/False Questions

F (page 297)　　　　1. In all cultures, men are naturally more aggressive than women.

F (page 294)　　　　2. Gender socialization begins when children enter school.

T (page 297)　　　　3. Gender roles vary greatly from culture to culture.

F (page 298)　　　　4. There are only two genders in all known societies.

T (page 299)　　　　5. There is no known society in which women are more powerful than men.

T (page 300)　　　　6. Since 1970, women have increased their participation in traditionally male jobs.

F (page 303)　　　　7. The gender pay gap has narrowed so considerably that men and women now earn the same amount of money for the same type of work.

F (page 319)　　　　8. Gender inequalities are inevitable and unchangeable.

F (page 319)　　　　9. Gender inequality is best understood as a separate issue from class and race.

T (page 323)　　　10. Structures of shared motherhood (kinship, neighborhood, and other networks of women) among African Americans have weakened in recent years.

Essay Questions

1. Discuss the influence of nature and nurture in the formation of gender identities. What are the arguments that biology primarily shapes gender? What are the sociological views on gender socialization? Summarize your conclusions about this fundamental question regarding gender.

2. If sex refers to *biological* differences, how could it be argued that sex, like gender, is socially constructed? Elaborate.

3. Compare and contrast gender roles in your country with those among a) the tribes of New Guinea studied by Margaret Mead; b) the !Kung; c) the Vanatinai; or d) indigenous societies that include multiple gender roles, such as the *berdache.*

4. What have been the trends in women's participation in the labor force in the United States since the early 1900s? How do you account for these trends? Have they resulted in economic equality between men and women? Explain.

5. How do traditional gender roles regarding housework and the raising of children affect women's employment status? How do these roles affect their life choices and living conditions?

6. Discuss the sociological research on differences in the treatment of boys and girls in education. What are the causes and effects of this treatment?

7. Outline the functionalist approaches to gender inequality of Murdock, Parsons, and Bowlby. How do feminists assess these approaches?

8. Summarize the explanations provided for gender inequalities by the three main feminist approaches discussed in the text: liberal, radical, and black feminism. Be sure to cover what each approach sees as the causes of and solutions to gender inequality. Bonus question: Discuss these perspectives in the context of the international women's movement.

9. Put yourself in the shoes of Andrea Ellington, the woman described in Chapter 10. How might you use sociology to understand and deal with the situations she faces in her life?

10. Apply the sociological understanding you have gained from this chapter to discuss your own gender identity—how you have acquired it, and your life chances as they are affected by your gender.

CHAPTER 11

Ethnicity and Race

Multiple-Choice Questions

d (page 332)

1. Stereotypes
   a. are usually fixed and inflexible categories.
   b. are systematic generalizations about a group based on limited information about part of that group.
   c. can be changed through education and experience.
   d. All of the above
   e. None of the above

c (page 333)

2. As a sociological concept, race refers to
   a. a set of distinct physical characteristics that are the basis for a scientific classification of human beings.
   b. the four clearly defined groups into which humans are easily categorized.
   c. physical variations in human beings singled out by members of a community or society as socially significant.
   d. All of the above
   e. None of the above

b (page 333)

3. _____ is a set of social relationships which allow individuals and groups to be located, and various attributes or competencies assigned, based on biologically grounded features.
   a. Ethnicity
   b. Race
   c. Class
   d. Nationality
   e. Religion

b (page 333)

4. Historically, Europeans classified individuals they came into contact with in various parts of the world according to categories based on their physical attributes. These categories became the basis of systems that shaped and constrained the peoples' daily lives. This process is known as
   a. genesis.
   b. racialization.
   c. ethnic cleansing.
   d. socialization.
   e. None of the above; this type of process never occurred in history.

b (pages 333–334)

5. As a sociological concept, ethnicity refers to
   a. a set of distinct physical characteristics that are the basis for a scientific classification of human beings.
   b. cultural practices and outlooks, including language, history, ancestry, religion, and styles of dress or adornment that tend to set people apart.
   c. an inborn difference that separates one group from others.
   d. All of the above
   e. None of the above

a (pages 334–335)

6. When people adopt an identity in some contexts but not in others they are practicing
   a. situational ethnicity.
   b. symbolic ethnicity.
   c. race.
   d. individual racism.
   e. institutional racism.

b (page 335)

7. When people assimilate into the larger culture but occasionally participate in ethnic customs they are practicing
   a. situational ethnicity.
   b. symbolic ethnicity.
   c. race.
   d. individual racism.
   e. institutional racism.

a (page 335)

8. Preconceived opinions or attitudes held by members of one group toward another are defined as
   a. prejudice.
   b. discrimination.
   c. racism.
   d. situational ethnicity.
   e. symbolic racism.

b (page 335)

9. Behavior that disqualifies members of one group from opportunities available to others is
   a. prejudice.
   b. discrimination.
   c. racism.
   d. situational ethnicity.
   e. symbolic racism.

c (page 336)

10. Prejudice based on socially significant physical distinctions is
    a. symbolic prejudice.
    b. discrimination.
    c. racism.
    d. situational ethnicity.
    e. symbolic racism.

d (page 336)

11. Racism that is not simply the opinions of a small segment of the population, but systematically pervades all of a society's structures and operations, is known as
    a. prejudice
    b. discrimination
    c. new racism
    d. institutional racism
    e. ethnicity

c (page 336)

12. According to some scholars, biologically based racism has been replaced by _____, which uses cultural differences to exclude certain groups.
    a. prejudice
    b. discrimination
    c. new racism
    d. institutional racism
    e. ethnicity

c (page 337)

13. _____, thinking in terms of fixed and inflexible
categories, often involves the psychological mechanism of
_____, directing hostility or anger toward objects that
are not really the source of those feelings.
   a. Institutional racism; situational ethnicity
   b. Symbolic ethnicity; individual racism
   c. Stereotypical thinking; displacement
   d. Scapegoating; projection
   e. Logic; rationality

b (page 337)

14. People who are blamed for things that are not their fault are
called
   a. racists.
   b. scapegoats.
   c. individual racists.
   d. authorities.
   e. scapesheep.

d (page 337)

15. _____ often involves _____, the unconscious
attribution to others of one's own desires or characteristics.
   a. Institutional racism; situational ethnicity
   b. Symbolic ethnicity; individual racism
   c. Stereotypical thinking; displacement
   d. Scapegoating; projection
   e. Logic; rationality

e (page 338)

16. In the 1940s, Theodor Adorno and his colleagues studied
the _____, a character type which was highly
prejudiced against Jews and other minorities, was rigidly
conformist and intolerant in religious and sexual attitudes.
   a. individual racist
   b. institutional racists
   c. scapegoat
   d. turncoat
   e. authoritarian personality

c (page 338)

17. Suspicion of outsiders and a tendency to judge other
cultures in terms of one's own cultural standards is called
   a. resource allocation.
   b. ethnic-group closure.
   c. ethnocentrism.
   d. individual racism.
   e. authoritarian personality.

b (page 338)

18. When an ethnic group maintains boundaries between itself and other groups, such as prohibiting intermarriage or creating physical separation between the groups, it is engaging in
    a. resource allocation.
    b. ethnic-group closure.
    c. ethnocentrism.
    d. individual racism.
    e. symbolic ethnicity.

a (page 339)

19. Early Marxists saw racism as a product of _____, who used it to exploit labor.
    a. the capitalist ruling class
    b. individual racists
    c. racist workers
    d. biologists
    e. archaeologists

a (page 343)

20. The systematic, planned destruction of a racial, political, or cultural group is called
    a. genocide.
    b. assimilation.
    c. segregation.
    d. pluralism.
    e. multiculturalism.

c (page 343)

21. In several parts of the former Yugoslavia, certain ethnic groups were subjected to harassment, threats, and campaigns of terror in order to forcibly expel them and create ethnically homogeneous regions. This practice is known as
    a. genocide.
    b. assimilation.
    c. ethnic cleansing.
    d. pluralism.
    e. ethnic integration.

c (page 344)

22. _____ is the physical separation of a racial or ethnic group.
    a. Genocide
    b. Assimilation
    c. Segregation
    d. Pluralism
    e. Multiculturalism

b (page 344)　　　23. When a group takes over the attitudes and language of the dominant community they have engaged in
 a. genocide.
 b. assimilation.
 c. segregation.
 d. pluralism.
 e. multiculturalism.

d (page 344)　　　24. _____ is a situation in which ethnic cultures have a distinct and separate existence while their members participate in the economic and political life of the larger society.
 a. Genocide
 b. Assimilation
 c. Segregation
 d. Pluralism
 e. Multiculturalism

e (page 344)　　　25. When ethnic groups have achieved a distinct but equal status, the society is said to exhibit
 a. genocide.
 b. assimilation.
 c. segregation.
 d. pluralism.
 e. multiculturalism.

e (pages 341–342)　26. Where were the major population flows in the period of Western expansion?
 a. from Europe to North America
 b. from Europe to South America
 c. from Europe to Africa and Austral-Asia
 d. from Africa to the Americas
 e. All of the above

d (page 342)　　　27. Why has racism thrived in the period since European expansion into the rest of the world?
 a. As cultural symbols, white and black have long been seen as opposites in European culture, with white representing purity and black symbolizing evil.
 b. The concept of race itself was invented and spread by Europeans in the eighteenth and nineteenth centuries.
 c. Racism was needed to justify the exploitation of nonwhite peoples by Europeans.
 d. All of the above
 e. None of the above

a (page 345)

28. Global migratory patterns are a result of the combination of _____, the movement of people *into* a country to settle, and _____, the process by which people leave a country to settle in another.
   a. immigration; emigration
   b. emigration; immigration
   c. assimilation; segregation
   d. segregation; assimilation
   e. social movement; colonialism

a (page 345)

29. The _____ model of immigration results in a "nation of immigrants."
   a. classic
   b. colonial
   c. guest workers
   d. illegal
   e. None of the above; "nation of immigrants" is a misnomer.

c (page 346)

30. Which of the following would be a *micro-level* factor that might be part of a systems approach to explaining migration patterns between Mexico and the United States?
   a. the U.S. policy encouraging "guest workers" from Mexico to work in American service industries
   b. economic conditions in Mexico that make it very difficult for many people to earn an adequate income
   c. informal networks among family and friends that provide support for newly arrived immigrants
   d. All of the above
   e. None of the above

d (page 347)

31. Dispersal of an ethnic population from an original homeland into foreign areas, often in a forced way or under traumatic circumstances is known as
   a. genocide.
   b. assimilation.
   c. pluralism.
   d. diaspora.
   e. emigration.

c (page 349) 32. More than 99 percent of the people in the United States are descended from
  a. Europeans.
  b. Africans.
  c. immigrants.
  d. Native Americans.
  e. Asians.

a (page 350) 33. The first large wave of immigrants to the United States, from the time of independence until the 1880s, were mostly from
  a. Britain and northwestern Europe.
  b. Eastern Europe.
  c. southern Europe.
  d. Asia.
  e. Latin America.

d (page 350) 34. Driven by a series of potato famines, 1.5 million people migrated to the United States from _____ in the nineteenth century, settling mostly in _____ areas.
  a. Germany; rural
  b. Germany; urban
  c. Ireland; rural
  d. Ireland; urban
  e. Poland; remote

b (page 350) 35. A large influx of people from _____ migrated to the United States in the 1880s and 1890s.
  a. Britain
  b. southern and eastern Europe
  c. northwestern Europe
  d. Asia
  e. Latin America

d (page 350) 36. Which of the following immigrant groups was subjected to prejudice and discrimination by those who were already established in the United States?
  a. Irish
  b. Italians
  c. Chinese
  d. All of the above
  e. None of the above

b (page 353)

37. Industrial development in the North and the mechanization of agriculture in the South resulted in a substantial migration of _____ to northern urban areas during the twentieth century.
   a. Europeans
   b. African Americans
   c. Latin Americans
   d. Native Americans
   e. Asians

d (page 353)

38. Which group has lived in the United States longer than all other immigrant groups besides Anglo-Saxons, yet still faces the segregation and poverty that for the other groups was only a transitional phase?
   a. Eastern Europeans
   b. southern Europeans
   c. Irish
   d. African Americans
   e. Asian Americans

a (page 353)

39. What Supreme Court decision established the foundation for the civil rights struggles of the 1950s–1970s?
   a. *Brown v. Board of Education of Topeka, Kansas*
   b. *Darwin v. Board of Education of the State of Kansas*
   c. *Roe v. Wade*
   d. *Clay v. Liston*
   e. *King v. City of Montgomery, Alabama*

d (page 354)

40. The majority of immigrants to the United States in 1900 were from _____; in 1990 the majority were from _____.
   a. Asia; Asia
   b. Europe; Europe
   c. Latin America; Europe and Asia
   d. Europe; Latin America and Asia
   e. Asia; Haiti

a (page 353)

41. What did the 1964 Civil Rights Act do?
   a. It banned discrimination in public facilities, education, employment, and any agency receiving government funds.
   b. It eliminated resistance to civil rights once and for all.
   c. It eliminated discrimination on the basis or race or ethnicity in the United States.
   d. All of the above
   e. None of the above

d (page 356)

42. If current U.S. population trends continue, _____ will outnumber _____ within the next decade.
    a. Irish Americans; German Americans
    b. African Americans; Irish Americans
    c. African Americans; Latinos
    d. Latinos; African Americans
    e. all ethnic minorities; whites

d (page 356)

43. Which of the following ethnic groups come from countries whose territories were at least partially conquered by the United States?
    a. Mexicans
    b. Puerto Ricans
    c. Native Americans
    d. All of the above
    e. None of the above

c (page 357)

44. Which ethnic group was forcibly removed to "relocation camps" in World War II?
    a. German Americans
    b. Italian Americans
    c. Japanese Americans
    d. All of the above
    e. None of the above

d (page 357)

45. Which of the following is a fact regarding racial and ethnic inequality in the United States today?
    a. Since the Civil Rights movement of the 1960s, increasing numbers of African Americans have joined the middle class by attaining a college education, professional occupations, and new homes.
    b. Blacks are much more likely than whites to live in poverty and be socially isolated from good schools and economic opportunity.
    c. Immigrants from Mexico seek economic opportunity but have among the lowest levels of educational attainment of all groups, and many live in extreme poverty.
    d. All of the above
    e. None of the above

b (page 360)

46. Which of the following groups saw the most significant *increase* in household family income in the 1990s?
    a. European Americans
    b. African Americans
    c. Hispanics
    d. Asian Americans
    e. None of the above; nobody's income increased significantly.

c (page 361)

47. What would be the most effective policy to eliminate racial and ethnic inequality in health, according to Jake Najman's (1993) research?
    a. more health education
    b. increased access to health care services
    c. attack poverty and reduce the income gap between rich and poor
    d. All of the above
    e. None of the above

a (page 361)

48. Douglas Massey and Nancy Denton (1993) argued that _____ is responsible for the continuation of black poverty in the urban ghettos of the United States.
    a. the history of racial residential segregation
    b. the genetic makeup of whites and blacks
    c. the culture of poverty
    d. All of the above
    e. None of the above

b (page 366)

49. What does Robert Blauner suggest as the best explanation for the significant difference between the least and most fortunate groups in the United States?
    a. the most fortunate have superior cultural attributes
    b. the least fortunate were originally present as colonized peoples rather than willing immigrants
    c. the least fortunate have inferior levels of intelligence and motivation
    d. All of the above are equally important factors.
    e. None of the above is true.

a (page 366)

50. Who argued that race has declined in its significance for blacks, especially with respect to economic disadvantages for the poorest segment of the community?
    a. William Julius Wilson
    b. the Association of Black Sociologists
    c. David Wellman
    d. Robert Blauner
    e. David Duke

b (page 367)

51. As studies by David Wellman (1987) and Douglas Massey and Nancy Denton (1993) have shown, _____ persists, even though _____ appears to be markedly reduced.
    a. overt prejudice; institutional racism
    b. institutional racism; overt prejudice
    c. overt prejudice; ethnic discrimination
    d. All of the above have significantly decreased.
    e. None of the above has significantly decreased.

True/False Questions

T (page 333)

1. There are no clear-cut biological races of human beings.

T (page 334)

2. Ethnic differences are learned behaviors.

F (pages 335–336)

3. An individual must be prejudiced in order to discriminate.

T (page 336)

4. "English only" laws would be an example of *new racism,* also known as cultural racism.

F (page 344)

5. The model of ethnic group relations that best describes the United States is multiculturalism.

T (page 358)

6. While more African Americans are now attending college, a much higher proportion of whites than blacks graduate.

F (page 358)

7. The unemployment rate of black and Hispanic men has shrunk since the 1960s, so it is now about the same as the unemployment rate for white men.

F (page 361)

8. There are few disparities in terms of the health of members of different racial and ethnic groups in the United States.

T (page 362)   9. On average, white male high school dropouts make more
                     money than black female college graduates.

T (pages 367–368) 10. Although both individual and institutional racism seem to
                      be declining in the United States, the differences between
                      white and nonwhite ethnic groups are long enduring.

Essay Questions

1. What does it mean when sociologists refer to skin color as a "master status"? In
   what ways is this phenomenon maintained and sustained in society today?

2. Why is race ultimately an unrealistic and unworkable concept? Why is it
   nonetheless a persistent way of categorizing people? Be sure to demonstrate your
   understanding of the *sociological* approach to these issues.

3. Racial distinctions are not merely abstract categories, according to the text, "they
   are also important factors in the reproduction of patterns of power and inequality
   within society." Explain this statement, and cite specific historic and
   contemporary examples of these patterns of power and inequality.

4. What is the difference between race and ethnicity? Do both of these concepts
   have their basis in culture? Explain.

5. What is the difference between prejudice and discrimination? How are they both
   related to racism and institutional racism?

6. What is so new about "new racism"?

7. How does prejudice operate, psychologically speaking? Discuss the processes of
   stereotypical thinking, displacement, scapegoating, projection, and the
   authoritarian personality type.

8. Discuss the sources and causes of ethnic conflict in the world over the past few
   decades. How do these conflicts compare with those of past historical periods?

9. Compare and contrast the four models of migration describing global population
   movements since 1945.

10. Explain the persistence of racial inequality in the United States despite significant
    declines in the overt expression of hostile attitudes of prejudice and racism. Refer
    specifically to the research by Blauner, Wilson, Wellman, and Massey and
    Denton in your response.

CHAPTER 12

Aging

Multiple-Choice Questions

e (page 372)

1. Average life expectancy in the world today is
   a. less than twenty years.
   b. twenty-two years.
   c. forty years.
   d. fifty-five years.
   e. sixty-five years.

c (page 372)

2. The average life expectancy for all Americans was _____ for those born in 1900, but is _____ for those born today.
   a. sixty; seventy
   b. seventy; sixty
   c. forty-seven; seventy-six
   d. seventy-five; forty-five
   e. thirty-five; eighty-two

a (page 372)

3. What accounts for most of the difference in life expectancy in the United States now compared to one hundred years ago?
   a. better chances that young people will survive
   b. better chances that middle aged people will survive
   c. better chances that old people will survive
   d. Life is more dangerous now than it was then, primarily because of higher crime rates.
   e. higher mortality rates now due to war and terrorism

b (page 374)

4. The number of Americans older than sixty-five will _____ between now and 2030.
   a. shrink by half
   b. more than double
   c. decline only slightly
   d. more than triple
   e. None of the above; it is impossible to predict such things.

e (page 374)

5. The discipline concerned with the study of the social aspects of aging is known as
   a. social aging.
   b. aging chronology.
   c. ageology.
   d. elder studies.
   e. social gerontology.

e (page 374)

6. Which of the following is the *sociological* definition of aging?
   a. the biological processes that affect people as they grow older
   b. the psychological processes that affect people as they grow older
   c. the social processes that affect people as they grow older
   d. the biological and social processes that affect people as they grow older
   e. the biological, psychological, and social processes that affect people as they grow older

c (page 375)

7. Which age consists of the norms, values, and roles that are culturally associated with a particular chronological point in a person's life?
   a. biological age
   b. psychological age
   c. social age
   d. normal age
   e. age role

d (page 374)

8. Biological aging usually involves
   a. declining vision.
   b. hearing loss.
   c. accumulation of fat, especially around the middle.
   d. All of the above
   e. None of the above; all of these are social stereotypes and are not inevitable.

e (page 375)

9. Psychological aging inevitably involves
   a. memory loss.
   b. a decline in learning ability.
   c. Alzheimer's disease.
   d. All of the above
   e. None of the above are inevitable; research suggests that psychological aging is a more complicated process.

d (page 375)   10. Alzheimer's disease
                       a.   is the primary cause of dementia in old age.
                       b.   is relatively rare in persons over seventy-five who are
                            in independent living situations.
                       c.   may be found in half of all people over eighty-five.
                       d.   All of the above
                       e.   None of the above

e (page 376)   11. Elderly people in the United States are likely to be
                       viewed as
                       a.   a source of historical memory.
                       b.   a source of traditional wisdom.
                       c.   productive and independent.
                       d.   All of the above
                       e.   None of the above

c (page 375)   12. "Act your age!" What age does this command refer to?
                       a.   biological age
                       b.   psychological age
                       c.   social age
                       d.   any age older than the one you are
                       e.   normal age

d (page 375)   13. In which of the following countries would an older person
                       most likely be revered as a source of wisdom and historical
                       memory?
                       a.   Japan
                       b.   China
                       c.   United States
                       d.   *a* and *b*
                       e.   *b* and *c*

d (page 375)   14. Role expectations for the elderly vary
                       a.   from one time period to another.
                       b.   from one culture to another.
                       c.   from one country to another.
                       d.   All of the above
                       e.   None of the above

a (page 376)

15. According to 1950s functionalist theorist Talcott Parsons,
    a. U.S. society needed to find roles for the elderly that were appropriate to their diminished physical and psychological capacities.
    b. elderly people needed to organize social movements to struggle for greater economic equality.
    c. older people should actively participate in shaping and defining their own social roles.
    d. All of the above
    e. None of the above

b (page 376)

16. Which theory explicitly argues that it is functional for society to remove elderly people from their roles to free those roles for others who would be more successful and productive?
    a. Talcott Parsons's functionalism
    b. disengagement theory
    c. activity theory
    d. conflict theory
    e. third-generation theories

d (page 376)

17. For whom is disengagement functional, according to the theory?
    a. the elderly, who are able to take on less demanding roles
    b. the young, who are able to fill roles abandoned by the elderly
    c. society, which benefits from the greater energy and new skills of the youth
    d. All of the above
    e. None of the above

b (page 377)

18. Which theory is vulnerable to the critique that it is based on stereotypical assumptions about the abilities of the elderly?
    a. biological aging theory
    b. disengagement theory
    c. activity theory
    d. conflict theory
    e. third-generation theories

c (page 377) 19. Both society and the elderly can benefit if elderly people remain actively engaged in work and other social roles as long as they can. Which theory advocates this position?
a. Talcott Parsons's functionalism
b. disengagement theory
c. activity theory
d. conflict theory
e. third-generation theories

e (page 377) 20. According to its critics, functionalist theory
a. focused too much on social inequalities and not enough on the abilities of the elderly.
b. paid too little attention to the inevitable mental and physical decline of the elderly.
c. unrealistically assumed the elderly could play an active part in defining their own role.
d. had no support in research.
e. emphasized the need for the elderly to adjust to existing conditions, rather than participate in changing them.

c (page 377) 21. The second generation of theories of aging focused on
a. how well the elderly were integrated into the larger society.
b. the extent to which activity is functional for the elderly and for society.
c. how the larger social structure creates unequal opportunities for the elderly, creating potential for social conflict.
d. All of the above
e. None of the above

a (page 377) 22. What is the source of many of the problems of aging, according to social conflict theories?
a. social institutions which favor those who have the most economic power
b. disengagement of the elderly from their previous roles
c. the self-concept of the elderly
d. All of the above
e. None of the above

d (page 377)   23. Who among the elderly fared worst in the 1980s, according to social conflict theorists?
    a. women
    b. low-income people
    c. minorities
    d. All of the above fared worse than others because of the combined effects of age, race, class, and gender.
    e. None of the above fared any worse than other elderly people.

b (page 378)   24. According to _____ theories, approaches popular in the 1950s and '60s, as well as those of the 1970s and '80s, overemphasized the importance of social structures in shaping the lives of the elderly.
    a. first-generation
    b. third-generation
    c. social conflict
    d. fifth-generation
    e. disengagement

d (pages 377–378)   25. Recent theories on aging emphasize
    a. ways that the elderly play active roles in determining their own physical and mental welfare.
    b. the role the elderly play in shaping their own living situation and self concept.
    c. increasing diversity among the elderly, including in how they age differently depending on their particular circumstances.
    d. All of the above
    e. None of the above

d (page 379)   26. Which of the following groups is more likely to live longer in U.S. society?
    a. black men
    b. white men
    c. black women
    d. white women
    e. None of the above; life expectancy is essentially the same regardless of sex or race.

d (page 379)

27. Which group is most likely to experience poor health, isolation, and economic insecurity?
    a. young-old
    b. old-old
    c. middle-old
    d. oldest old
    e. None of the above is more likely to have those problems than the others.

a (page 380)

28. Social Security provides the average retiree
    a. approximately 40 percent of his or her income.
    b. 100 percent of his or her income.
    c. a lifestyle below the poverty line.
    d. a life of luxury.
    e. less than 20 percent of his or her income.

b (page 380)

29. Largely because of Medicare and Social Security, poverty rates among the elderly in the United States have _____ over the past thirty years.
    a. decreased only slightly
    b. declined steadily and significantly
    c. increased slightly
    d. increased steadily and significantly
    e. stayed about the same

d (page 381)

30. Research in the United States shows
    a. a significant desire and willingness of adult children to maintain contact with and financially support their parents, if necessary.
    b. many elderly parents continue to support their children, especially in times of difficulty.
    c. most elderly people with children live close to at least one of them.
    d. All of the above
    e. None of the above

b (page 382)

31. Among the elderly, which group is more likely to have problems of isolation and loneliness?
    a. men, because they are less sociable than women
    b. women, because they are more likely to outlive husbands and have more difficulty finding another mate
    c. young-old women, because they are young enough to remember companionship, but too old to enjoy it
    d. Both men and women are equally likely to experience loneliness.
    e. None of the above; since age is so highly valued today, elderly people are rarely alone.

a (page 383)

32. Which of the following is illegal in the United States?
    a. discrimination on the basis of age
    b. prejudice against the elderly
    c. andragogy
    d. All of the above
    e. None of the above

b (page 383)

33. Prejudice and/or discrimination based on age is
    a. illegal.
    b. ageism.
    c. no longer a problem in the United States.
    d. All of the above
    e. None of the above

d (page 383)

34. Which of the following is a source of ageism?
    a. stereotypes of the elderly as sad, lonely, and senile
    b. the obsession with youth in American popular culture
    c. new technology, like computers, that the elderly may be unfamiliar with
    d. All of the above
    e. None of the above

e (page 383)

35. Physical abuse of the elderly
    a. is common.
    b. is more likely to be committed by their children than by their spouse.
    c. is unconnected with financial dependence.
    d. All of the above
    e. None of the above

d (page 386)

36. Regarding the health of the elderly in the United States:
    a. The incidence of chronic disabilities has declined in recent years.
    b. Most elderly people think their own health is relatively good.
    c. Elderly patients account for around one third of health care expenditures.
    d. All of the above
    e. None of the above

a (page 386)

37. With respect to health care, how do the elderly differ from other age groups in the United States?
    a. They are almost all covered by government funded health insurance.
    b. They are remarkably less likely to suffer from health problems.
    c. They are fortunate not to be afflicted with new diseases, like HIV/AIDS.
    d. All of the above
    e. None of the above

e (page 386)

38. Which of the following countries does NOT provide full health care coverage for their elderly?
    a. Canada
    b. France
    c. Sweden
    d. Germany
    e. United States

e (page 386)

39. A 1997 survey found that Americans' worst fear about growing old is
    a. having nothing to do.
    b. death.
    c. being lonely.
    d. becoming a financial burden on others.
    e. living for many years in a nursing home.

c (page 387)

40. What term is used by educators to refer to adult learning?
    a. pedagogy
    b. demagogy
    c. andragogy
    d. geragogy
    e. hereyagogy

b (page 387)

41. Andragogy and geragogy are most likely to emphasize
    a. artificial intelligence.
    b. building on the extensive life experience of older learners.
    c. formal, traditional methods of teaching.
    d. All of the above
    e. None of the above

d (page 388)

42. Why do the elderly have such a strong political voice in the U.S. government?
    a. they are growing in numbers
    b. they have high voter turnout, accounting for up to one-fifth of the vote
    c. they have an effective organization representing their interests in the AARP
    d. All of the above
    e. None of the above; the elderly are actually quite politically weak.

b (page 388)

43. Which program covers the cost of acute medical care for the elderly?
    a. Medicaid
    b. Medicare
    c. Social Security
    d. TANF
    e. AMC

a (page 388)

44. Which program covers medical care for the poor and long term care (nursing homes) for the elderly when they have "drawn down" or spent most of their assets (except their homes)?
    a. Medicaid
    b. Medicare
    c. Social Security
    d. TANF
    e. AMC

c (page 388)

45. Which program provides retirement pay for all elderly persons who have worked at least a minimum number of years in their lifetime?
    a. Medicaid
    b. Medicare
    c. Social Security
    d. TANF
    e. AMC

a (page 388)

46. The average monthly benefit for recipients of Social Security
    a. provides a minimal level of support, barely enough to get by.
    b. keeps most elderly persons below the poverty level.
    c. is higher for women than for men, since the former usually have higher expenses.
    d. All of the above
    e. None of the above

c (page 389)

47. By 2050, _____ of the population in industrialized societies will be age sixty-five and over.
    a. 5 percent
    b. 14 percent
    c. 25 percent
    d. 50 percent
    e. 68 percent

b (page 389)

48. Striking a balance between the needs and interests of different generations is called
    a. gerontocracy.
    b. generational equity.
    c. andragogy.
    d. geragogy.
    e. the generation gap.

c (page 389)

49. The question of generational equity will become more acute as
    a. an increasingly poor elderly population is supported by an increasingly wealthy younger cohort.
    b. the proportion of the elderly in the population continues to shrink.
    c. fewer and fewer people of working age pay more and more in taxes to support elderly retirees.
    d. All of the above
    e. None of the above

d (page 389)

50. The combination of the graying of the population and globalization will mean
    a. traditional patterns of family care will be challenged.
    b. a probable increased burden on government support programs for the elderly.
    c. challenges to traditional ways of thinking and behaving toward the elderly.
    d. All of the above
    e. None of the above

True/False Questions

T (page 372) 1. If elderly people have rich and stimulating lives, it is likely their mental abilities will not decline significantly until their late eighties.

F (page 376) 2. Old people are helpless victims of role expectations for the elderly.

T (page 377) 3. Activity theory is supported by research that shows enhanced mental and physical health for elders who stay engaged in their work as long as they are able.

F (page 379) 4. In U.S. society, the elderly are generally a homogenous group with little variation in physical and mental ability, class, political values, or sexual preference.

F (page 379) 5. Among the elderly in the United States, the "oldest old" are most likely to be economically independent.

T (page 380) 6. Social Security and Medicare have kept many elderly people out of poverty.

T (page 380) 7. Race is a more significant factor than age in poverty among the elderly in the United States.

F (page 381) 8. The majority of the elderly in the United States are socially isolated.

F (page 383) 9. It is easier for women than men to grow old gracefully because of U.S. cultural values.

F (page 388) 10. The elderly are so similar in their political views that, unlike other age groups, they can be represented by a single organization, the American Association for the Advancement of Retired Persons (AARP).

Essay Questions

1. What are the important differences between chronological age and social age? Which is more likely to be affected by culture? Explain.

2. Discuss, in detail, the meaning of the phrase, "the graying of America".

3. Apply each of the following theories to the situation of an elderly person you know: activity theory, disengagement theory, conflict theory.

4. What is the key difference between the most recent theories about the elderly and previous functionalist and conflict theories? Do these new theories make sense in relation to elderly people you know? Explain.

5. Like other forms of prejudice, ageism is increasingly anachronistic. Explain why.

6. Discuss the issue of *generational equity*. Do the elderly receive more or less of society's resources than they should? Justify your position in terms of your personal values and interests, making reference to empirical facts and trends.

7. As the twenty-first century progresses, fewer working-age people are paying taxes to support programs for the elderly. How do you think this situation can be resolved?

8. How can the lifelong learning needs of a graying population best be met?

9. How will the lives of the elderly worldwide be affected by the combined processes of "graying" and globalization?

10. In relation to changes discussed in this chapter, how do you envision your own life when you are sixty-five? seventy-five? eighty-five?

CHAPTER 13

Government, Political Power, and Social Movements

Multiple-Choice Questions

b (page 394)　　　　1.　_____ is the term for the regular enactment of policies, decisions, and matters of state on the part of officials within a political apparatus.
　　　　a.　State
　　　　b.　Government
　　　　c.　Politics
　　　　d.　Power
　　　　e.　Authority

c (page 394)　　　　2.　_____ is the means whereby power is used to affect the scope and content of governmental activities.
　　　　a.　State
　　　　b.　Government
　　　　c.　Politics
　　　　d.　Sovereignty
　　　　e.　Authority

d (page 394)　　　　3.　All political life is about
　　　　a.　the state.
　　　　b.　the government.
　　　　c.　sovereignty.
　　　　d.　power.
　　　　e.　authority.

d (page 394)　　　　4.　The ability of individuals or groups to make their own interests or concerns count, even when others resist, is
　　　　a.　state.
　　　　b.　government.
　　　　c.　politics.
　　　　d.　power.
　　　　e.　authority.

e (page 394) 5. Which term refers to the legitimate use of power?
   a. state
   b. government
   c. politics
   d. power
   e. authority

a (page 394) 6. Where there is a political apparatus ruling over a given territory, whose authority is backed by a legal system and by the capacity to use military force to implement its policies, a _____ exists.
   a. state
   b. government
   c. politics
   d. power
   e. authority

a (page 394) 7. Which of the following is a characteristic of a traditional state?
   a. poorly defined territories
   b. high degree of sovereignty
   c. people living within the borders are citizens
   d. All of the above
   e. None of the above

d (page 395) 8. Which of the following is a characteristic of a nation-state?
   a. a government apparatus with sovereign rights within the borders of a territory
   b. able to back its sovereignty by control of military power
   c. many citizens have positive feelings of commitment based on nationalism
   d. All of the above
   e. None of the above

d (page 395) 9. Which of the following statements is true about nationalism?
   a. It gives people a sense of pride and belonging as part of a single political community.
   b. As an identity with a distinct, sovereign community, it only arose with the modern state.
   c. Nationalistic loyalties do not always correspond with the boundaries of states.
   d. All of the above
   e. None of the above

c (page 395)

10. Of the types of rights associated with the growth of citizenship, _____ refer to the rights of individuals in law.
   a. social rights
   b. political rights
   c. civil rights
   d. left rights
   e. right rights

b (page 395)

11. Of the types of rights associated with the growth of citizenship, _____ refer to the right to take part in such things as elections and running for office.
   a. social rights
   b. political rights
   c. civil rights
   d. left rights
   e. right rights

a (page 398)

12. Of the types of rights associated with the growth of citizenship, _____ refer to the right of every individual to enjoy a certain minimum standard of economic welfare and security.
   a. social rights
   b. political rights
   c. civil rights
   d. left rights
   e. right rights

a (page 398)

13. In most countries, _____ were the last to develop, based in large part on the exercise of the other two.
   a. social rights
   b. political rights
   c. civil rights
   d. left rights
   e. right rights

b (page 398)

14. When social rights become broadly established and government agencies provide material benefits for those who are unable to support themselves, a _____ is said to exist.
   a. nation-state
   b. welfare state
   c. state of anarchy
   d. social state
   e. laissez-faire state

b (page 398)   15. What is the basic meaning of democracy?
                     a. free enterprise
                     b. "the people" rule
                     c. whoever is in charge rules
                     d. monarchs rule
                     e. seniors rule

a (page 399)   16. In a _____ decisions are made directly and communally
                     by those affected by them.
                     a. participatory democracy
                     b. constitutional monarchy
                     c. liberal democracy
                     d. one-party Communism
                     e. the two-party system

b (page 402)   17. A _____ exists where a king or queen continues to
                     exercise some governmental authority, if only symbolic,
                     but is limited by a constitution which vests authority in the
                     elected representatives of the citizens.
                     a. participatory democracy
                     b. constitutional monarchy
                     c. liberal democracy
                     d. one-party Communism
                     e. the two-party system

b (page 402)   18. Why have liberal democratic systems spread so rapidly
                     since 1989, according to the text?
                     a. People care less about wealth and capitalism
                         nowadays, and more about politics.
                     b. Globalization tends to influence people's lives more
                         now, leading them to push for more information about
                         how they are governed, and thus for more democracy.
                     c. Communication systems are still restricted in most
                         parts of the world, so people are more interested in
                         their own, local affairs and less concerned about what
                         is happening elsewhere.
                     d. All of the above
                     e. None of the above

d (page 403)

19. What do we call an organization of individuals, with broadly similar political aims oriented towards achieving legitimate control of government through an electoral process?
    a. liberal democracy
    b. participatory democracy
    c. Communism
    d. political party
    e. constitutional monarchy

a (page 403)

20. Where is one likely to find a two-party liberal democracy, rather than one in which five, six, or more parties are represented?
    a. where elections are based on the principle of "winner-takes-all"
    b. where elections result in proportional representation
    c. in a Communist society
    d. All of the above
    e. None of the above

e (page 403)

21. Which system is more likely to result in political parties that converge on the "middle ground" and often come to resemble each other so closely that there is little distinctive difference in their key policies?
    a. multi-party system
    b. constitutional monarchy
    c. participatory democracy
    d. one-party Communism
    e. two-party system

a (page 404)

22. Which system allows diverse interests and points of view to be expressed more directly, and provides room for representation of more radical alternatives?
    a. multiparty system
    b. constitutional monarchy
    c. participatory democracy
    d. one-party Communism
    e. two-party system

b (page 404)

23. Which is an example of a two-party system?
    a. European parliaments
    b. the United States
    c. the Soviet Union
    d. China
    e. None of the above

c (page 405)

24. What is an interest group?
    a. a political party
    b. an alliance of banks to establish common fees
    c. an organization that attempts to influence elected officials to consider their aims when deciding on legislation
    d. the capability of individuals and groups to make their own interests count, even when others resist
    e. None of the above

d (page 405)

25. What do lobbyists do?
    a. try to get officials to support a vote in favor of their cause
    b. make campaign contributions
    c. get paid high salaries
    d. All of the above
    e. None of the above

b (page 406)

26. What theory of the nature and limits of modern democracy was developed by Max Weber and Joseph Schumpeter?
    a. pluralism
    b. democratic elitism
    c. the power elite
    d. All of the above
    e. None of the above

d (pages 406–407)

27. What is necessary for effective democracy in modern, large, bureaucratic states, according to Max Weber?
    a. a large substratum of bureaucrats who have the expertise to run the government
    b. parties that represent different interests and have different outlooks
    c. courageous and imaginative political leaders
    d. All of the above
    e. None of the above

b (page 408)

28. Joseph Schumpeter argued that democracy is the rule of
    a. the people.
    b. the politician.
    c. the monarch.
    d. the pope.
    e. None of the above

a (page 408) 29. What theorists, influenced by Max Weber and Joseph
Schumpeter, argue that interest groups limit the
concentration of power in the hands of government
officials?
a. pluralists
b. democratic elitists
c. constitutional monarchists
d. power elitists
e. interested parties theorists

d (page 408) 30. A unified group of people in the highest positions of the
federal government, the large corporations, and the military
runs the United States and exercises tremendous influence
in the world, according to C. Wright Mills. What is this
group called?
a. pluralist theorists
b. the democratic elite
c. the constitutional monarchy
d. the power elite
e. the New World Order

d (page 412) 31. The overthrow of an existing political order by means of a
mass movement, using violence, is a
a. social movement.
b. collective behavior.
c. riot.
d. revolution.
e. coup d'état.

a (page 412) 32. A collective attempt to further a common interest or secure
a common goal through action outside the sphere of
established institutions is a
a. social movement.
b. collective behavior.
c. riot.
d. revolution.
e. coup d'état.

a (page 413)   33. The primary source of the contradictions that lead to class struggle and revolution is _____, in Marx's model.
    a. change in the forces of production
    b. change in the minds of the bourgeoisie
    c. change in the minds of the proletariat
    d. the political system
    e. religion

b (page 413)   34. According to Marx, _____ is "the motor of history" or the primary factor in social change.
    a. free will
    b. class struggle
    c. the great man
    d. hate
    e. the V-8

d (page 413)   35. According to James Davies, a sense of _____ in times of improving living conditions and _____ leads to protest and revolution.
    a. absolute deprivation; falling expectations
    b. absolute deprivation; rising expectations
    c. relative deprivation; falling expectations
    d. relative deprivation; rising expectations
    e. relative expectations; rising deprivation

e (page 414)   36. Which of the following is a component of collective action, according to Charles Tilly?
    a. organization
    b. mobilization
    c. common interests
    d. opportunity
    e. All of the above

a (page 415)   37. Theda Skocpol believes revolutions are _____ of the more limited aims of different groups.
    a. unintended consequences
    b. intended outcomes
    c. inevitable results
    d. All of the above, depending on the situation
    e. None of the above; she doesn't believe in revolution.

d (pages 415–416)   38. What would be an example of structural strain in Smelser's terms?
  a. uncertainties about goals
  b. clashes of goals
  c. persistent inequalities between ethnic groups
  d. Any of the above
  e. None of the above

b (page 417)   39. Touraine's concept of "historicity" means
  a. one must understand the past of urban areas in order to understand the present.
  b. there are more social movements in the modern world because individuals and groups know that social activism can be used to achieve social goals and reshape society.
  c. social movements generally thrive on people who are totally out of control of their emotions.
  d. All of the above
  e. None of the above

b (page 421)   40. Seen as a unique product of late modern society, _____ differ significantly in methods, motivations, and orientations from the collective action of earlier times.
  a. liberal democracies
  b. new social movements
  c. old social movements
  d. nation-states
  e. welfare states

e (pages 421–422)   41. In recent years, participants in social movements have shown an ability to do something that is particularly worrisome to governments. This is the ability to
  a. organize big petition drives in major metropolitan centers.
  b. use photocopiers to print large numbers of leaflets.
  c. make phone calls to their elected representatives.
  d. charter buses to transport demonstrators to rallies.
  e. coordinate international political campaigns using the Internet and other technology.

a (page 400)   42. Which of the following contributed to the "wave of
                    democracy" in the 1980s and '90s?
                    a. globalization
                    b. nuclear proliferation
                    c. the Cold War
                    d. All of the above
                    e. None of the above

b (page 402)   43. Why do corporations prefer to do business in democratic
                    states, according to the text?
                    a. Corporations have an inherent philosophical
                        preference for democracy.
                    b. Democracies tend to be more stable than other states,
                        enhancing the possibility for profit.
                    c. Corporations are not allowed to do business with
                        dictatorships.
                    d. All of the above
                    e. None of the above; corporations do not prefer
                        democracies, according to the text.

True/False Questions

T (page 394)   1. Power is a factor in almost all social relationships.

T (page 394)   2. Dictatorships are based on authority if their citizens see
                    them as legitimate.

T (page 394)   3. All modern societies are nation-states.

F (page 394)   4. Most nation-states came into being as a result of the
                    political participation of their citizens.

F (page 399)   5. The political system in ancient Greece was a liberal
                    democracy.

T (page 404)   6. Both of the two major political parties in the United States
                    have been in decline since the 1950s in terms of level of
                    membership and voting support.

F (page 406)   7. Women in the United States have gained more power in government than they have in business.

T (page 408)   8. C. Wright Mills argued that political power in the United States is controlled by a power elite.

T (pages 424–425)   9. According to Gellner, the nation-state is a product of modern, industrialized society.

F (page 426)   10. It is impossible to have a nation without a state.

Essay Questions

1. What is the difference between the *government* and the *state?* Apply these concepts to describe the political structure in your country.

2. What is the difference between *power* and *authority?* Provide a detailed example of each from your own experience.

3. Discuss the three types of rights that develop with the growth of citizenship. Explain how such rights are manifested in your country?

4. Define and give examples of each of the following: participatory democracy, constitutional monarchy, and liberal democracy.

5. Discuss the global spread of democratic ideals in the 1980s and 1990s. Do you think this "wave of democracy" will continue to spread in the first half of the twenty-first century? Why or why not?

6. *Who Rules America?* is the title of a book in which William Domhoff applies and updates C. Wright Mills's theory of the power elite. How would you respond to the question, "Who rules America?" Would you use democratic elitism, pluralism, or the power elite as your theoretical basis? Justify your choice. How would you explain the role of interest groups? Women? Campaign contributions? Is democracy in America in trouble?

7. Compare and contrast the theories of state overload and legitimation crisis. Do you see support for either of these theories in the conditions of the early twenty-first century?

8. Are you, or is anyone you know, a participant in a social movement? If so, how would you classify the movement, using categories discussed in Chapter 13? Justify your answer by referring to specific characteristics with which you are familiar.

9. Apply one of the social movement theories (economic deprivation, resource mobilization, structural strain, fields of action, or new social movements) to the feminist movement. Choose either the first phase (nineteenth century) or the "resurgence" phase which began in the late twentieth century. Bonus: Explain *both* phases, using *two different* theories.

10. What is the connection between globalization, nationalism, and social movements today?

CHAPTER 14
Work and Economic Life

Multiple-Choice Questions

a (page 434)

1. Carrying out tasks requiring the expenditure of mental and physical effort in order to produce goods and services that cater to human needs would be termed
   a. work.
   b. occupation.
   c. income.
   d. wealth.
   e. Taylorism.

b (page 434)

2. Work done in exchange for a regular wage or salary is
   a. work.
   b. an occupation.
   c. a wager.
   d. wealth.
   e. Taylorism.

b (page 434)

3. Institutions that provide for the production and distribution of goods and services make up the
   a. family.
   b. economy.
   c. political system.
   d. religion.
   e. technology.

e (page 435)

4. The harnessing of science to machinery in order to achieve greater productive efficiency is known as
   a. family.
   b. economy.
   c. political system.
   d. religion.
   e. technology.

d (pages 435–436)
5. Work provides _____, which in turn tends to structure people's psychological makeup and daily lives.
   a. money
   b. personal identity
   c. social contacts
   d. All of the above
   e. None of the above

d (page 436)
6. Transactions outside the sphere of regular employment, sometimes involving the exchange of cash for services, but often involving direct exchange of goods or services are said to make up the
   a. family.
   b. economy.
   c. political system.
   d. informal economy.
   e. technology.

c (page 436)
7. From a sociological perspective, women who are housewives
   a. don't have a job.
   b. want a job.
   c. do *work*, although they are not part of the paid labor force.
   d. go shopping all day.
   e. spend a lot of time with their friends.

a (page 436)
8. Work has become divided into a number of different occupations in which people specialize. Sociologists refer to this as
   a. the division of labor.
   b. self-provisioning.
   c. occupational division.
   d. occupational segregation.
   e. technology.

b (page 437)
9. In the larger traditional societies there were 20–30 major craft trades, and most people were
   a. metal workers.
   b. self-sufficient.
   c. economically interdependent.
   d. All of the above
   e. None of the above

c (page 437)

10. In modern societies there are thousands of occupations, and therefore a great deal of
    a. tailorism.
    b. self-sufficiency.
    c. economic interdependence.
    d. All of the above
    e. None of the above

d (page 437)

11. An American management consultant named _____ invented a system of _____, in which industrial processes were studied in order to break them down into precisely timed and organized simple operations.
    a. Henry Ford; Taylorism
    b. Henry Ford; Fordism
    c. Frederick Winslow Taylor; Fordism
    d. Frederick Winslow Taylor; scientific management
    e. Homer Winslow; Simpson management

d (page 437)

12. Taylorism resulted in
    a. the loss of workers' control over knowledge of the production process.
    b. reduced autonomy of craft workers from management.
    c. deskilling and degrading of labor.
    d. All of the above
    e. None of the above

b (page 438)

13. The system developed by _____, in which mass production is tied to the cultivation of mass markets, is known as _____.
    a. Henry Ford; Taylorism
    b. Henry Ford; Fordism
    c. Frederick Winslow Taylor; Fordism
    d. Frederick Winslow Taylor; scientific management
    e. Homer Winslow; Simpson management

c (page 438)

14. According to Karl Marx, capitalism reduces many people's work to dull, uninteresting tasks, over which workers have no influence or control. What term did he use to refer to this situation and the feelings it engendered?
    a. self-provisioning
    b. informal economy
    c. alienation
    d. the division of labor
    e. scientific management

c (page 438)

15. Jobs that are set by management, geared toward machines, and over which workers have little control—in short, are alienating—are referred to as
   a. self-provisioning.
   b. high-trust systems.
   c. low-trust systems.
   d. occupations.
   e. work.

b (page 438)

16. Jobs where workers control the pace and content of their work, within general guidelines, are referred to as
   a. self-provisioning.
   b. high-trust systems.
   c. low-trust systems.
   d. occupations.
   e. work.

d (page 439)

17. What is a temporary stoppage of work by a group of employees in order to express a grievance or enforce a demand called?
   a. self-provisioning
   b. lockout
   c. absenteeism
   d. strike
   e. riot

c (page 440)

18. From 1950 to 1980, _____—the number of union members as a percentage of the number of people who could potentially be union members—declined in most of the developed countries.
   a. the Taylor ratio
   b. the Ford ratio
   c. union density
   d. the division of labor
   e. the multiplication of labor

d (page 442)

19. Which of the following characterizes capitalism as a way of organizing economic life?
   a. private ownership of the means of production
   b. profit as incentive
   c. free competition in markets
   d. All of the above
   e. None of the above

a (page 442)

20. Which economic system involves restless expansion and investment to accumulate capital?
    a. capitalism
    b. socialism
    c. social democracy
    d. communism
    e. cumulus system

c (page 442)

21. Since the turn of the twentieth century, capitalist economies have been increasingly dominated by
    a. communists
    b. socialists
    c. corporations
    d. entrepreneurs
    e. labor unions

b (page 442)

22. The _____—the boss who owns and runs the firm—is still common in thousands of _____ in the American economy.
    a. communist; government agencies
    b. entrepreneur; smaller firms
    c. entrepreneur; big corporations
    d. communist; big corporations
    e. entrepreneur; government agencies

d (page 442)

23. Which of the following statements about the U.S. economy is true?
    a. The two hundred largest manufacturing corporations control over half of all manufacturing assets.
    b. The two hundred largest financial organizations control over half of all financial activity.
    c. Financial institutions hold over 30 percent of the shares of the two hundred largest manufacturing companies.
    d. All of the above
    e. None of the above

a (page 443)

24. Which stage of corporate capitalism is dominated by large firms run by individual entrepreneurs or their family members and passed on to their descendants?
    a. family capitalism
    b. managerial capitalism
    c. institutional capitalism
    d. communism
    e. socialism

c (page 443)

25. When one firm is in a commanding position in an industry it is a(n)
    a. low-trust system.
    b. high-trust system.
    c. monopoly.
    d. public company.
    e. oligopoly.

e (page 443)

26. When a small group of giant corporations predominate in an industry they constitute a(n)
    a. low-trust system.
    b. high-trust system.
    c. monopoly.
    d. public company.
    e. oligopoly.

b (page 444)

27. In which stage of corporate capitalism is the company itself a more defined economic entity, separate from the entrepreneurial family, and controlled by managers?
    a. family capitalism
    b. managerial capitalism
    c. institutional capitalism
    d. communism
    e. socialism

a (page 444)

28. According to Jacoby, "welfare capitalism"
    a. was a paternalistic model in which corporations controlled workers through "moral education."
    b. disappeared in the 1930s.
    c. reappeared in the 1960s in the form of government subsidies to corporations.
    d. All of the above
    e. None of the above

c (page 444)

29. Which stage of corporate capitalism is based on the practice of corporations owning shares in other firms, with interlocking directorates controlling much of the corporate landscape?
    a. family capitalism
    b. managerial capitalism
    c. institutional capitalism
    d. communism
    e. socialism

c (page 444)

30. What type of corporate capitalism is dominant today?
    a. family capitalism
    b. managerial capitalism
    c. institutional capitalism
    d. communism
    e. socialism

c (page 445)

31. Large corporations that have branches in two or more countries are referred to as
    a. family capitalism.
    b. managerial capitalism.
    c. transnational corporations.
    d. communists.
    e. entrepreneurs.

b (page 445)

32. What has made possible the tremendous increase in transnational corporations over the past thirty years?
    a. the dominance of family capitalism
    b. advances in transportation and communications
    c. the elimination of poverty in the Third World
    d. All of the above
    e. None of the above

a (page 445)

33. While there is now an _____, it is dominated by _____.
    a. international division of labor; international oligopolies
    b. international family capitalism; an international division of labor
    c. ethnocentric division of labor; international family capitalism
    d. All of the above
    e. None of the above

c (pages 445–446)

34. When a transnational corporation has its headquarters in its country of origin and companies and plants in other countries are cultural extensions of the original, it is called
    a. family capitalism.
    b. managerial capitalism.
    c. an ethnocentric transnational.
    d. a polycentric transnational.
    e. a geocentric transnational.

d (page 446)   35. When the headquarters of a transnational sets broad
                    guidelines but the local companies manage their own
                    affairs it is called
                    a. family capitalism.
                    b. managerial capitalism.
                    c. an ethnocentric transnational.
                    d. a polycentric transnational.
                    e. a geocentric transnational.

e (page 446)   36. When the managerial systems of a corporation are
                    integrated on a global basis, and higher managers are very
                    mobile among the countries in which it operates, it is called
                    a. family capitalism.
                    b. managerial capitalism.
                    c. an ethnocentric transnational.
                    d. a polycentric transnational.
                    e. a geocentric transnational.

c (page 446)   37. Which country has the most ethnocentric transnationals,
                    according to H.V. Perlmutter?
                    a. United States
                    b. United Kingdom
                    c. Japan
                    d. Germany
                    e. Russia

a (page 446)   38. Images and dreams are spread throughout the world, even
                    to the Third World, through movies, TV programs, music,
                    videos, games, toys, and T-shirts. Richard Barnet and John
                    Cavanagh call this the
                    a. Global Cultural Bazaar.
                    b. Global Shopping Mall.
                    c. Global Workplace.
                    d. Global Financial Network.
                    e. Global Positioning Satellite.

b (page 446)   39. The poor don't have the resources to participate in the
                    _____, according to Richard Barnet and John
                    Cavanagh.
                    a. Global Cultural Bazaar
                    b. Global Shopping Mall
                    c. Global Workplace
                    d. Global Financial Network
                    e. Global Positioning Satellite

c (page 446)

40. Richard Barnet and John Cavanagh refer to the international division of labor as the
   a. Global Cultural Bazaar.
   b. Global Shopping Mall.
   c. Global Workplace.
   d. Global Financial Network.
   e. Global Positioning Satellite.

d (page 446)

41. Billions of bits of information stored in computers, tracking an endless stream of currency exchanges, credit card transactions, insurance plans, and the buying and selling of stocks and bonds make up the _____, according to Richard Barnet and John Cavanagh.
   a. Global Cultural Bazaar
   b. Global Shopping Mall
   c. Global Workplace
   d. Global Financial Network
   e. Global Positioning Satellite

b (page 448)

42. Although some large corporations are still strongly centralized bureaucracies based in the United States, most today are
   a. smaller than they used to be.
   b. more like an "enterprise web," with decentralized operations across the globe.
   c. investing in factories and equipment in the United States that produce tangible products.
   d. All of the above
   e. None of the above

d (page 448)

43. Where might a Pontiac Le Mans be made?
   a. Detroit
   b. South Korea
   c. Germany
   d. All of the above
   e. None of the above

b (page 448)

44. The proportion of workers in the industrialized countries who work in blue-collar occupations has
   a. steadily risen in the past fifty years.
   b. progressively fallen in the past fifty years.
   c. stayed about the same in the past fifty years.
   d. totally disappeared in the past fifty years.
   e. None of the above; there never were blue collar workers in the industrialized countries.

b (page 456)

45. The "new" economy—in which ideas, information, and forms of knowledge support and sustain innovation and growth—is most commonly called
   a. the idea economy.
   b. the knowledge economy.
   c. the informative stage.
   d. the flim-flam order.
   e. the thin air economy.

a (page 448)

46. _____ is the process of replacing human labor power with programmable machines, or _____.
   a. Automation; robots
   b. Robota; automats
   c. Globalization; high-trust systems
   d. Alienation; robots
   e. None of the above

a (page 449)

47. Which sociologist sees the implementation of automation in the workplace as a way to reduce the alienation experienced by workers?
   a. Robert Blauner
   b. Harry Braverman
   c. Shoshana Zuboff
   d. Richard Sennet
   e. Steven Spielberg

c (page 450)

48. In a 1983 review of the literature on "the skill debate," Spenner found that
   a. most jobs have been "deskilled."
   b. most jobs have been "upskilled."
   c. jobs have been "upskilled" in terms of their complexity of tasks, but "deskilled" in terms of control of their work by the workers.
   d. skill levels have remained essentially unchanged.
   e. the notion of "skill" in most jobs has been always overrated.

a (page 451)

49. The general process of using collaborative work groups instead of production lines is known as
   a. group production.
   b. quality circles.
   c. deskilling.
   d. upskilling.
   e. None of the above

a (page 451)

50. An example of _____ is _____, groups of between five and twenty workers who meet regularly to resolve production problems.
   a. group production; quality circles
   b. quality circles; group production
   c. deskilling; upskilling
   d. upskilling; deskilling
   e. None of the above

d (page 454)

51. This question was composed on a Dell computer, the author purchased by selecting the specific features he wanted on the company's Web site and placing the order there. Dell's method is the prime model of the production system known as
   a. Fordism.
   b. Taylorism.
   c. Dellism.
   d. mass customization.
   e. mass confusion.

True/False Questions

F (page 434)

1. Work possesses little social significance.

T (page 435)

2. Job conditions, such as the opportunity to work in jobs that are challenging, not routinized, and not subject to close supervision, are known to affect a person's sense of self-worth.

F (page 437)

3. Frederick Winslow Taylor invented the moving assembly line.

F (page 438)

4. Fordism provides an inexpensive way to provide the flexibility needed for specialized markets.

T (page 440)

5. Labor unions originate as a way of redressing the imbalance of power between workers and their employers.

T (page 445)

6. Half of the largest economic units in the world today are transnational corporations.

F (page 449)   7. The introduction of computerized technology in the
                         workplace has improved the job conditions of all workers.

T (pages 454–455)   8. Much of the clothing that we buy today was likely made in
                         foreign sweatshops by young workers—most likely
                         teenage girls—who get paid relatively low wages.

F (page 455)   9. The occupational structure remained basically the same
                         throughout the twentieth century.

T (page 458)   10. Researchers estimate that contingency workers include
                         between 25 and 33 percent of the American workforce.

Essay Questions

1. Chapter 14 opens with the stories of two workers at a General Motors auto
   assembly plant who faced major choices in adapting to the reorganization of that
   factory in the late 1980s. Edward Salermo chose to get further education and new
   skills, and after a few changes in direction is still seeking an improvement in his
   current job with another company. Susan Roberts stayed with GM but was
   disappointed with the kinds of "improvements" the company initiated. What
   sociological concepts and theories introduced in the chapter help you make sense
   of their dilemmas and choices?

2. Work plays an important role in structuring people's lives. Yet Marx, in the
   nineteenth century, argued that work in modern industrial society (capitalism) is
   inherently alienating. Discuss the significance of Marx's concept in light of more
   recent research on work and the economy in late modern society.

3. What is Fordism? How is it connected with unions and collective bargaining
   agreements through a "virtuous circle"? Why do most sociologists think it broke
   down in the 1970s?

4. Why did union density grow in most developed countries between 1950 and
   1980, then decline after that period?

5. Discuss the findings of the Worker Representation and Participation Survey
   (WRPS). What was the population of the study? What did Freeman and Rogers
   find is the thing workers want most? Were there any indications that workers are
   satisfied with attempts to meet that desire? Explain.

6. What is "welfare capitalism"? What were the assumptions and practices of welfare capitalism from the end of the nineteenth century until the 1930s? How was it adapted and changed in subsequent years?

7. One way to approach globalization is in terms of a developing "international division of labor." What, exactly, is meant by that phrase? How does that global structure affect workers in the developed countries? In the developing countries?

8. Does the "knowledge economy" really make money "from thin air," as Charles Leadbeater says? What makes that kind of "production" possible? What is the connection between the knowledge economy and older economic sectors, such as agriculture, mining, and agriculture? Where does the knowledge economy fit in the international division of labor?

9. Discuss the debate about automation among sociologists and industrial relations experts over the past fifty years. Summarize the positions of Blauner, Braverman, and Zuboff regarding alienation, deskilling, and the double-edged nature of information technology. How does Spenner synthesize these disparate views?

10. Why is it more difficult to introduce mass customization in the auto industry than it was in the computer industry? Compare GM's initial approach with that of Dell. How are car manufacturers trying to adapt to those difficulties?

CHAPTER 15
Families and Intimate Relationships

Multiple-Choice Questions

b (page 467)

1. What is the term for a group of persons directly linked by kin connections, the adult members of which assume responsibility for caring for children?
   a. kinship
   b. family
   c. marriage
   d. community
   e. nation-state

a (page 467)

2. Connections between individuals, established either through marriage or through the lines of descent that connect blood relatives, are known as
   a. kinship.
   b. family.
   c. marriage.
   d. community.
   e. nation-state.

c (page 467)

3. A socially acknowledged and approved sexual union between two adult individuals is called
   a. kinship.
   b. family.
   c. marriage.
   d. community.
   e. nation-state.

a (page 467)

4. Two adults living together in a household with their own or adopted children would be a(n)
   a. nuclear family.
   b. extended family.
   c. atomic family.
   d. distended family.
   e. polyandry.

b (page 467)

5. A(n) _____ is one in which close relatives other than just a married couple and their children live in the same household or in a close and continuous relationship with one another.
   a. nuclear family
   b. extended family
   c. atomic family
   d. distended family
   e. polyandry

c (page 467)

6. A family of orientation is
   a. one formed by two married adults and their children by previous marriages.
   b. a family a person wishes to belong to.
   c. the family into which a person is born.
   d. the family which one enters as an adult and within which a new generation of children is brought up.
   e. None of the above

d (page 467)

7. A family of procreation is
   a. one formed by two married adults and their children by previous marriages.
   b. a family a person wishes to belong to.
   c. the family into which a person is born.
   d. the family which one enters as an adult and within which a new generation of children is brought up.
   e. None of the above

a (page 467)

8. The situation in which a married couple lives in or very near the home of the bride's parents is called
   a. matrilocal.
   b. patrilocal.
   c. neolocal.
   d. polygamy.
   e. polyandry.

b (page 467)

9. If a married couple lives near or with the parents of the groom the pattern is called
   a. matrilocal.
   b. patrilocal.
   c. neolocal.
   d. polygamy.
   e. polyandry.

a (page 467)   10. If it is illegal for a man or a woman to be married to more than one individual at a time, a system of _____ exists.
      a.   monogamy
      b.   polygamy
      c.   polygyny
      d.   polyandry
      e.   mononucleosis

b (page 467)   11. A marriage system that allows a husband or wife to have more than one spouse is called
      a.   monogamy.
      b.   polygamy.
      c.   polygyny.
      d.   polyandry.
      e.   mononucleosis.

c (page 467)   12. If a man is allowed to have more than one wife, the marriage system is
      a.   monogamy.
      b.   polygamy.
      c.   polygyny.
      d.   polyandry.
      e.   mononucleosis.

d (page 467)   13. _____ exists when a woman may be married to more than one man at a time.
      a.   Monogamy
      b.   Polygamy
      c.   Polygyny
      d.   Polyandry
      e.   Mononucleosis

a (page 468)   14. Which analyst sees the family as meeting the social needs for primary socialization and personality stabilization?
      a.   Talcott Parsons
      b.   Betty Friedan
      c.   Ann Oakely
      d.   Ulrich Beck
      e.   Betty Crocker

e (page 468)

15. According to functionalists, the husband in the "conventional family" is the breadwinner and plays the _____ role, while the wife cares for the home and children and plays the _____ role.
    a. major; minor
    b. supporting; leading
    c. nuclear; extended
    d. mechanical; organic
    e. instrumental; affective

c (page 468)

16. Which perspective has been most concerned with the domestic division of labor, unequal power relationships, and caring activities in the family?
    a. functionalism
    b. Marxism
    c. feminism
    d. instrumentalism
    e. fundamentalism

b (page 471)

17. _____ is (are) the basis of marriages formed through personal selection, based on affection or love.
    a. Arranged marriages
    b. Affective individualism
    c. Nuclear families
    d. Extended families
    e. Polygamies

d (page 472)

18. Which of the following characteristics could be found within the "traditional" American family in the period from colonial times to the 1950s?
    a. exceedingly harsh discipline over children
    b. a sexual double standard (promiscuity for men; strict sexual restrictions for women)
    c. widespread dissatisfaction among women
    d. All of the above
    e. None of the above; the traditional family was a model of peace and harmony.

d (page 472)   19. Why are family systems in the Third World changing?
                          a.   the spread of Western culture, especially the ideal of
                               romantic love
                          b.   the development of central governments, which
                               actively try to alter traditions
                          c.   massive migration from rural to urban areas
                          d.   All of the above
                          e.   None of the above

a (page 473)   20. Which of the following is an aspect of change affecting
                          family systems worldwide?
                          a.   Clans and other kinship groups are declining in
                               influence.
                          b.   There is less sexual freedom than there used to be.
                          c.   Children have fewer rights than they used to.
                          d.   All of the above
                          e.   None of the above

b (page 488)   21. When couples live together without being married they are
                          engaging in
                          a.   engagement.
                          b.   cohabitation.
                          c.   an illegal act.
                          d.   All of the above
                          e.   None of the above

d (pages 474–476)   22. What accounts for the trend toward later marriages in
                          recent decades?
                          a.   increases in cohabitation
                          b.   increased participation of women in the labor force
                          c.   decrease in the numbers of "marriageable men"
                               because of economic deterioration
                          d.   All of the above, combined with other variables
                          e.   None of the above has anything to do with the timing
                               of marriage.

d (page 477)   23. The rate of cohabitation (unmarried couples sharing the
                          same household) has _____ since 1970.
                          a.   fallen slightly
                          b.   fallen steeply
                          c.   risen slightly
                          d.   risen steeply
                          e.   stayed the same

d (page 477)   24. What percentage of American children live in a household
                      in which the husband works for pay and the wife stays at
                      home, taking care of children and household?
                      a. 90 percent
                      b. 72 percent
                      c. 50 percent
                      d. 25 percent
                      e. 6 percent

d (pages 475–476) 25. Which of the following factors contributed to the current
                      fact that far fewer African-American women aged 25–44
                      are married and living with a husband than their white
                      counterparts?
                      a. historical conditions, including kinship customs in
                          sub-Saharan Africa and the subsequent effects of
                          slavery
                      b. discrimination and migration
                      c. conditions of poverty and unemployment in the inner
                          cities today
                      d. All of the above have combined effects on
                          contemporary cultural practices.
                      e. None of the above

a (page 478)   26. Which of the following is more likely to exhibit
                      characteristics of extended kinship?
                      a. African-American families
                      b. Colonial period white families
                      c. Victorian era white families
                      d. White families in the 1990s
                      e. None of the above exhibit extended kinship.

c (page 480)   27. Which Hispanic group has more wealth in family business
                      ownership, lower levels of fertility, and low levels of non-
                      marital fertility, compared with other Latinos?
                      a. Mexican Americans
                      b. Puerto Ricans
                      c. Cuban Americans
                      d. Salvadoreños
                      e. None of the above; Latino groups are pretty equal in
                          all these dimensions.

d (page 480)

28. Which group has a strong commitment to family interdependence, family and friend networks that help members financially, and higher median incomes than non-Hispanic whites?
    a. Mexican Americans
    b. Puerto Ricans
    c. Cuban Americans
    d. Asian Americans
    e. Native Americans

e (page 481)

29. Which group has the highest rate of intermarriage with other racial-ethnic groups?
    a. Mexican Americans
    b. Puerto Ricans
    c. Cuban Americans
    d. Asian Americans
    e. Native Americans

b (pages 481–482)

30. The _____ in the United States rose rapidly from the 1960s to the late 1970s, peaking in 1980.
    a. marriage rate
    b. divorce rate
    c. number of extended families
    d. All of the above
    e. None of the above

b (page 482)

31. Lenore Weitzman (1985) found that no-fault divorce had a negative unintended consequence for _____, decreasing their average income by 73 percent in the first year, while _____ saw their average income increase by 42 percent.
    a. men and their children; women
    b. women and their children; men
    c. men and women; children
    d. children; men and women
    e. None of the above; there were no negative consequences.

d (page 482)   32. Why have divorce rates risen over the last few decades?
                    a. Changes in the law have made getting a divorce easier.
                    b. Marriage has less to do with handing down property
                        and status from generation to generation today, except
                        for the wealthy.
                    c. Women are more economically independent now, and
                        marriage is less of an economic necessity for them.
                    d. All of the above
                    e. None of the above; divorce rates have declined since
                        the 1960s.

b (page 482)   33. Who is more likely to get a divorce at some point in their
                    life cycle?
                    a. people whose parents never divorced
                    b. people who cohabitate before marriage
                    c. people who marry at an older age
                    d. All of the above
                    e. None of the above

d (page 482)   34. Which of the following factors increases the likelihood that
                    a person will get a divorce at some point in their life?
                    a. premarital childbearing
                    b. a childless marriage
                    c. low income
                    d. All of the above
                    e. None of the above

c (page 483)   35. Diane Vaughan's 1986 study, *Uncoupling*, found that one
                    partner is often more dissatisfied with the relationship and
                    begins to explore her or his options, including separation or
                    divorce. She refers to this person as the
                    a. malcontent.
                    b. "bad guy."
                    c. initiator.
                    d. cause of the problem.
                    e. manipulator.

d (page 483)

36. Although their studies may not be representative of the population as a whole, Judith Wallerstein and her colleagues found that for children of divorced parents:
    a. all experienced emotional disturbance at the time of the divorce.
    b. two-thirds were coping reasonably well after five years.
    c. after fifteen years, nearly all felt they had suffered in some way from their parents' mistakes.
    d. All of the above
    e. None of the above

b (page 484)

37. For people in the same age group, who is more likely to get married?
    a. people who have never been married
    b. people who have been married and divorced
    c. poor people
    d. divorced women
    e. None of the above; all of the above are equally likely to get married.

e (page 484)

38. A family in which at least one of the adults is a stepparent is a(n)
    a. nuclear family.
    b. extended family.
    c. postmodern family.
    d. single-parent family.
    e. stepfamily.

e (page 484)

39. Regarding the general effects of divorce on children, Cherlin concludes that
    a. the majority experience serious mental health problems.
    b. most experience long-term problems that persist into adulthood.
    c. a minority resume normal development without serious problems within two years of the divorce.
    d. All of the above
    e. None of the above

b (page 485)

40. Research shows that _____ suffer more negative effects from stepfamily life while _____ suffer more negative effects from single-parent family life.
   a. boys; girls
   b. girls; boys
   c. boys; boys also
   d. girls; girls also
   e. None of the above; children do not experience negative effects from either situation.

a (page 485)

41. One in five families with dependent children are
   a. single-parent households.
   b. living in poverty.
   c. extended families.
   d. All of the above
   e. None of the above

a (page 487)

42. The age group most likely to be victims of child abuse is
   a. zero to three years.
   b. four to seven years.
   c. eight to ten years.
   d. eleven to fifteen years.
   e. sixteen years and above.

d (page 488)

43. What trend is apparent with respect to cohabitation?
   a. The number of couples who see cohabitation as an end in itself rather than a trial marriage is increasing.
   b. An increasing proportion of babies born "out of wedlock" are to cohabiting couples.
   c. Cohabitation as an alternative to marriage is increasing in Nordic countries, as well as in the United States.
   d. All of the above
   e. None of the above

d (page 488)

44. Most young people see cohabitation as
   a. incest.
   b. sexual abuse.
   c. domestic violence.
   d. "trial marriage."
   e. "absent father."

c (pages 490–491)   45. Today, more people _____ in order to _____, but
eventually 90 percent of them _____.
  a. get married; leave home; get divorced
  b. leave home; get married; leave home again to become
     independent
  c. leave home; start an independent life; get married
  d. get divorced; leave home; move back with their
     parents
  e. get married; drop out of school; end up as professors
     writing confusing exam questions

a (page 491)   46. David Popenoe believes the _____ is the cause of many
social problems in America.
  a. decline of the traditional family
  b. rise of the traditional family
  c. decline of the postmodern family
  d. All of the above
  e. None of the above

b (page 491)   47. Judith Stacey defines the "breadwinner-father and child
rearing-mother" as the
  a. traditional family.
  b. modern family.
  c. postmodern family.
  d. All of the above
  e. None of the above

d (page 475)   48. Arlie Hochschild found that _____ is creating pressure
on American workers to work longer hours than they used
to.
  a. ambition
  b. the mass media
  c. the education system
  d. globalization
  e. the booming economy

True/False Questions

F (page 467)   1. Monogamy is the most common form of marriage in the
world as a whole.

F (page 467)   2. The predominant form of the family in premodern western
Europe was the extended family.

F (page 472) 3. The American family of the colonial period was the model of stability, with most marriages lasting at least twenty-five years.

T (page 472) 4. The most dramatic increase in labor force participation among women after World War II occurred among married women with young children.

T (page 473) 5. In some places in the world, the extended family is being rejuvenated or taking new forms.

T (page 474) 6. The average age of first marriage has risen over the past twenty years.

T (page 479) 7. From the cultural viewpoint of some countries, such as Pakistan, the African-American family looks much more like what they would call a family than the typical white American family.

F (page 482) 8. Rising divorce rates indicate that people are increasingly dissatisfied with the whole idea of marriage.

T (page 483) 9. A continuing relationship with both parents following divorce helps children cope better with the separation.

T (page 488) 10. The trend of increasing rates of cohabitation started among lower-educated groups in the 1950s.

Essay Questions

1. In the past, marriage and the family had a primarily economic role. In modern societies, that role is replaced by intimacy communication as the foundation of the marriage relationship. Discuss the implications of this change in terms of the numerous other changes in marriage and the family that take place as societies continue to change and develop.

2. What is the feminist critique of the functionalist view of the "conventional" family and its specialized roles?

3. Why is love so important to people in late-modern society, according to Beck and Beck-Gernsheim? What do you think they mean by the title of their book, *The Normal Chaos of Love?*

4. Trace the changes that have occurred in the family as an institution over the past five hundred years. Focus particularly on Coontz's account of the history of the family in the United States since colonial times.

5. What is the evidence that American workers are working longer hours today than they did in the past? How is "the time bind" faced by "the overworked American" related to globalization?

6. What factors account for the trend toward later marriages in the United States in recent decades?

7. Discuss the particular characteristics of African-American families. Compare and contrast the explanations of these patterns by Moynihan; Morgan, et.al.; and Aschenbrenner.

8. What are the effects of divorce on children? You may draw on personal experience, but be sure to put it in the context of the range of sociological research on this topic.

9. "Violence within families is primarily a male domain," according to the text. How do you reconcile this statement with research by Straus that finds women reporting they commit about the same number of "violent acts" as men?

10. Describe the growing movement in Canada and the United States to recognize gay unions as marriages and provide homosexuals the same legal rights as heterosexual couples, including the right to form and maintain families with children.

CHAPTER 16

Education and the Mass Media

Multiple-Choice Questions

d (page 498)

1. A sociological analysis of education would include
   a. school as a socializing agent.
   b. the relationship between education and social inequality.
   c. the social functions that schools provide.
   d. All of the above
   e. None of the above

b (page 498)

2. For most people in premodern times, learning took place in
   a. school.
   b. the family.
   c. public.
   d. All of the above
   e. None of the above

c (page 498)

3. Modern education on a large scale emerged in the _____ century.
   a. seventeenth
   b. eighteenth
   c. nineteenth
   d. twentieth
   e. twenty-first

c (page 499)

4. As industrialization progressed and cities expanded, the education system
   a. deteriorated.
   b. remained mired in ancient ideas and beliefs.
   c. was expanded and developed to meet the increasingly technical and innovative needs of society and individual needs for occupational skills.
   d. All of the above
   e. None of the above

d (page 499)

5. Why did formal systems of education develop in modern societies?
   a. Mass education promoted nationalism, helping to integrate citizens from different regions and backgrounds into a national society.
   b. Schools promoted the development of personality traits, like self-discipline and obedience, that employers needed in their employees.
   c. Schools provide the credentials needed for a job, and credentialism reinforces the class structure in a society.
   d. All of the above
   e. None of the above

d (pages 522–523)

6. Globalization and technological innovations in telecommunication have made possible
   a. e-universities.
   b. Internet-based learning.
   c. a distance learning model that reproduces *online* the basic ingredients of traditional learning, such as group collaboration and individual attention from instructors.
   d. All of the above
   e. None of the above

a (page 500)

7. Jonathan Kozol's study of American schools found
   a. high levels of segregation within schools and great inequalities between them.
   b. that because of government funding, schools around the country spend the same amount per pupil.
   c. that tracking is a successful practice.
   d. that schools have no long-term impact on a person's success.
   e. that computers have had little impact on the educational system.

e (page 501)

8. James Coleman's extensive study of American schools in the 1960s found
   a. more differences in resources and facilities between predominantly white and predominantly African-American schools than he expected.
   b. that material differences in schools have the most significant effect on educational performance.
   c. that family and peer group influences had little effect on educational performance.
   d. All of the above
   e. None of the above

a (page 501)

9. _____ is the practice of dividing students into groups that receive different instruction on the basis of assumed similarities in their ability or attainment.
   a. Tracking
   b. Dividing
   c. Assimilating
   d. The hidden curriculum
   e. Credentialism

c (page 502)

10. Jeannie Oakes (1990) found that students placed in the "low achieving" group—mostly African-American, Latino, and poor students—received a _____ education as a result.
    a. somewhat better
    b. more equal
    c. poorer
    d. much better
    e. None of the above; she found no effect at all.

a (page 504)

11. To the extent that schools help perpetuate social and economic inequalities across generations, they are part of the process of
    a. social reproduction.
    b. social transformation.
    c. social revolution.
    d. All of the above
    e. None of the above

b (page 504)

12. Much of what is learned in school has nothing to do with the formal content of the lessons. The teaching of values, attitudes, and habits constitute the
    a. tracking system.
    b. hidden curriculum.
    c. credentialism.
    d. formal curriculum.
    e. social transformation.

c (page 505)

13. The hierarchical authority relations of schools parallel those of the _____, according to Samuel Bowles and Herbert Gintis.
    a. family
    b. prison
    c. workplace
    d. democratic system
    e. utopia

d (page 507)

14. Scores on IQ tests correlate highly with
    a. academic performance.
    b. economic differences.
    c. ethnic differences.
    d. All of the above
    e. None of the above

c (page 507)

15. In *The Bell Curve: Intelligence and Class Structure in American Life*, Richard J. Herrnstein and Charles Murray argue that the significant differences in IQ between various races and ethnic groups are explained by
    a. unequal opportunities.
    b. oppressive social conditions.
    c. genetic inheritance.
    d. All of the above
    e. None of the above

b (page 507)

16. Evidence that social advantage results in higher IQ scores _____ Richard J. Herrnstein's and Charles Murray's view on intelligence.
    a. supports
    b. refutes
    c. proves
    d. neither supports nor refutes
    e. None of the above; no such evidence exists.

d (page 511)

17. James Coleman's research on segregated schools resulted in the policy of _____, which provoked a lot of opposition, some of it violent.
    a. hidden curriculum
    b. credentialism
    c. savage inequalities
    d. busing
    e. trucking

a (page 512)

18. Proponents of school privatization are critical of public education because they believe
    a. it is wasteful and bureaucratic.
    b. not enough resources are devoted to administration.
    c. good teachers are too easily fired by jealous administrators.
    d. All of the above
    e. None of the above

d (page 512)

19. Critics of school privatization claim that
    a. companies like the Edison Project simply repackage the best innovations of public schools.
    b. such companies introduce technology like computers without demonstrating their connection with the curriculum.
    c. such companies are less interested in education reform than in making money for investors.
    d. All of the above
    e. None of the above

b (page 513)

20. A major legacy of colonialism is the high level of _____ in the Third World.
    a. literacy
    b. illiteracy
    c. primary education
    d. income
    e. wealth

a (page 513)

21. In traditional cultures, most knowledge was what the anthropologist Clifford Geertz called
    a. local knowledge.
    b. regional knowledge.
    c. general knowledge.
    d. useless knowledge.
    e. communication.

a (page 510)

22. In a counterargument to the claims made in *The Bell Curve*, a team of University of California-Berkeley sociologists asserted that _____ is more important than intelligence in determining how well people do in life.
    a. one's parents' socioeconomic status
    b. the number of students per classroom
    c. the success of busing
    d. one's SAT score
    e. None of the above

e (page 516)

23. When we talk about the transfer of information from one person, context, or group to another, we're talking about
    a. local knowledge.
    b. regional knowledge.
    c. general knowledge.
    d. useless knowledge.
    e. communication.

b (page 517)

24. According to Jürgen Habermas, the emergence of a _____ in industrial societies created a sphere of communication, where public opinion is formed and attitudes are molded.
    a. hidden curriculum
    b. public sphere
    c. local knowledge
    d. tracking system
    e. hyperreality

c (page 517)

25. The electronic media create a world in which people across the globe see major news events as they occur, and thereby participate together in the same events— _____, in Marshall McLuhan's terms.
    a. local knowledge
    b. regional knowledge
    c. a global village
    d. useless knowledge
    e. hyperreality

b (page 517)

26. The _____ undermines the _____, and thereby stifles democracy, according to Jürgen Habermas.
    a. local knowledge; regional knowledge
    b. culture industry; public sphere
    c. global village; hyperreality
    d. All of the above
    e. None of the above

e (page 518)

27. Jean Baudrillard argues that "reality" has been transformed by the mass media, and now exists as a _____ in which images on the TV screen intermingle with people's behavior.
   a. hidden curriculum
   b. public sphere
   c. local knowledge
   d. tracking system
   e. hyperreality

a (page 518)

28. In his theory of the media, John Thompson uses the term _____ to refer to dialogical interaction that is rich in clues that individuals can use to make sense of others' statements.
   a. face-to-face interaction
   b. mediated interaction
   c. mediated quasi-interaction
   d. communication
   e. hyperreality

b (page 518)

29. In his theory of the media, John Thompson uses the term _____ to refer to dialogical interaction that involves the use of a media technology, which stretches out the interaction over time and space.
   a. face-to-face interaction
   b. mediated interaction
   c. mediated quasi-interaction
   d. communication
   e. hyperreality

c (page 519)

30. In his theory of the media, John Thompson uses the term _____ to refer to monological interaction of the type created by the mass media, where people are not linked directly, but interact in an indirect way over time and space.
   a. face-to-face interaction
   b. mediated interaction
   c. mediated quasi-interaction
   d. communication
   e. hyperreality

a (page 520)

31. The _____ is an international system for the production, distribution, and consumption of information.
    a. world information order
    b. hyperreality
    c. mediated hyper-interaction
    d. information station
    e. information superhighway

a (page 520)

32. Like other aspects of the global society, information is dominated by the most powerful industrialized countries, especially the United States. This system is referred to as
    a. media imperialism.
    b. hyperreality.
    c. mediated hyper-interaction.
    d. information station.
    e. information superhighway.

e (page 520)

33. Herbert Schiller argues that _____ corporations and culture have become globally dominant by creating a "total corporate informational-cultural environment."
    a. British
    b. French
    c. Chinese
    d. Japanese
    e. U.S.

d (page 521)

34. Why has money become electronic and the stock exchange a 24-hour global market?
    a. constant improvements in computer technology
    b. the digitization of data, allowing integration of computer and telecommunications technologies
    c. satellite communication and fiber optics technologies
    d. All of the above
    e. None of the above; money is still money and the stock exchange is still a daytime operation.

a (page 523)

35. When you combine different media that used to require separate technologies you get
    a. multimedia.
    b. multitechnology.
    c. a computer.
    d. a satellite.
    e. confused.

b (page 520)

36. The Internet had its origins in 1969 as a project of
    a. Massachusetts Institute of Technology (MIT).
    b. the Pentagon.
    c. Bill Gates and Microsoft Corporation.
    d. All of the above
    e. None of the above

c (page 521)

37. The development of the graphical interface of the Internet, the World Wide Web, was initiated by
    a. the Pentagon.
    b. major corporations, like Microsoft.
    c. seemingly anonymous individuals, such as a software engineer at a Swiss lab and an American undergraduate student.
    d. Al Gore.
    e. Bill Gates.

e (page 521)

38. The "place" formed by the global network of computers where internet interaction takes place is called
    a. Yahoo!
    b. MSNBC.
    c. AOL.
    d. http.
    e. cyberspace.

d (page 522)

39. In terms of the impact of the Internet on social interaction, sociologists see
    a. new kinds of electronic interaction that enhance or add to face-to-face relationships.
    b. expanded and enriched social networks.
    c. increased social isolation and automation.
    d. All of the above
    e. None of the above

e (page 523)

40. Schools originally arose
    a. to meet the popular demand for education.
    b. as part of the administrative apparatus of the modern state, with a hidden curriculum to ensure discipline and control, according to Michel Foucault.
    c. largely as a result of the development of printing and the ensuing need for broader literacy.
    d. *a* and *b*
    e. *b* and *c*

204 | CHAPTER 16

d (page 523)

41. The increasing use of computer technology in education may result in
    a. the transformation of the existing curriculum.
    b. the development of a "classroom without walls."
    c. the "re-engineering" of schools, similar to the way businesses have been transformed by computer technology.
    d. All of the above
    e. None of the above

b (page 523)

42. Given the social structure in which computer technology is developing, _____ will likely reinforce material deprivation that already exists in some areas.
    a. the information superhighway
    b. information poverty
    c. hyperreality
    d. the classroom without walls
    e. the hidden curriculum

e (page 523)

43. Within developed countries,
    a. access to computers is widespread.
    b. computer use and skills are nearly universal.
    c. most sociologists think that information technology is responsible for increasing social equality.
    d. All of the above
    e. None of the above

d (page 523)

44. According to the 1999 UNDP *Human Development Report,*
    a. the knowledge economy is rapidly decreasing economic inequality between nations.
    b. the least developed nations are rapidly adopting information technology.
    c. there is no such thing as a "digital divide."
    d. Internet access has become the new line of demarcation between the rich and the poor.
    e. people in Africa will soon have as much access to the Internet as people in western Europe.

b (page 524)

45. New information technologies and the growth of the knowledge economy will affect education by
    a. undermining, and ultimately destroying, education as a formal institution.
    b. shifting the emphasis toward active, lifelong learning in a diversity of settings.
    c. further confining teaching and learning to traditional schools and colleges where the technology is located.
    d. transferring educational activities entirely to cyberspace.
    e. confining education to the young, who alone can understand the new technology.

d (page 507)

46. The Berkeley team of sociologists who critically analyzed *The Bell Curve* found that
    a. racial differences in intelligence are *not* biologically determined.
    b. racial differences in intelligence are socially caused.
    c. inequities in intelligence can be removed by implementing good social policies.
    d. All of the above
    e. None of the above

a (page 502)

47. Which country has the largest number of foreign students attending its colleges and universities?
    a. United States
    b. United Kingdom
    c. China
    d. Germany
    e. Russia

d (page 503)

48. What is the benefit of the exchange of international students?
    a. it plays a vital role in globalization
    b. cross-national understandings are enhanced
    c. xenophobic and isolationist attitudes are reduced
    d. All of the above
    e. None of the above

d (page 503)

49. Why is the internationalization of education considered problematic by some?
    a. Foreign students may deprive Americans from slots in competitive programs.
    b. Some foreign students receive financial aid and scholarships, taking money that might otherwise go to Americans.
    c. Foreign students are likely to return to their home countries and not contribute to American society.
    d. All of the above
    e. None of the above

d (page 503)

50. Supporters of international education suggest more should be done to encourage foreign students to come to the United States, because
    a. they often develop a sympathetic attitude toward the United States, and carry that attitude into their leadership in their homelands.
    b. most are supported by their parents, not by financial aid.
    c. they put hundreds of millions of dollars back into the U.S. economy.
    d. All of the above
    e. None of the above

True/False Questions

F (page 499)

1. Capitalists fought the development of mass public education, fearing that workers who could read would not work.

T (page 499)

2. One of the goals of providing universal access to education is to help reduce inequalities in wealth and power.

F (page 500)

3. Jonathan Kozol's best-selling book, *Savage Inequalities*, exposes the effects of the barbaric behavior of today's students.

F (page 504)

4. Sociological research has found that in all instances tracking is entirely negative in its effects.

F (page 506)   5. Paul Willis's study of working class youth in an English school showed how they ended up in dull, boring jobs because they lacked the skills and intellect to do anything else.

F (page 507)   6. Scientists have agreed on a simple definition of intelligence: the ability to solve abstract mathematical puzzles.

T (page 510)   7. *Burakumin* are genetically the same as other Japanese, but have lower IQ scores because of social inequalities.

F (page 517)   8. Jürgen Habermas argued that the Internet created the first "public sphere."

T (page 517)   9. Given current trends, the average child born today will have spent more time watching TV than engaged in any other activity, except sleeping, by the time she reaches the age of eighteen.

Essay Questions

1. Explain how technology has always been connected with education, and how technological change has led to changes in education.

2. How is the development and expansion of public education tied to the needs of an industrializing and urbanizing society?

3. Does education reduce or maintain inequality in society? Justify your answer with data and theories discussed in this chapter.

4. Discuss the concept of "intelligence" and attempts to measure it. Summarize the debate over the idea that IQ is genetically determined.

5. Why are private corporations and their investors interested in privatizing education? What are the implications of this development for the ultimate goals of education?

6. What are the connections between the rise of mass media and mass education? Apply Habermas's theory of communication and the public sphere to explain these connections.

7. Explain a topic receiving current extensive coverage in the mass media in terms of Baudrillard's concept of "hyperreality." Can Thompson's concepts of "mediated interaction" or "mediated quasi-interaction" also help make sense of the event? Explain.

8. What are the effects of the Internet on communication? Is the Internet part of the mass media? Explain.

9. What impact has the Internet had on education? What are the implications of the "digital divide" for social inequalities, both domestically and globally?

10. The text suggests that the idea of education as a formal institution is being replaced by the notion of lifelong learning. How does this fit with the traditional humanistic ideals of education? How will you be affected, personally, by these developments?

CHAPTER 17
Religion in Modern Society

Multiple-Choice Questions

b (page 528)

1. A cultural system of commonly shared beliefs and rituals that provides a sense of ultimate meaning and purpose by creating an idea of reality that is sacred, all encompassing, and supernatural would be termed _____ by sociologists.
   a. sociology
   b. religion
   c. theism
   d. philosophy
   e. realism

d (page 528)

2. The sociological definition of religion includes elements of
   a. culture.
   b. behavior.
   c. a sense of the purpose and meaning of life.
   d. All of the above
   e. None of the above

b (page 529)

3. Belief in one or more supernatural deities is called
   a. religion.
   b. theism.
   c. animism.
   d. evangelism.
   e. Buddhism.

b (page 529)

4. Which of the following questions about religion is sociological?
   a. Is it true or false?
   b. What are its principal beliefs and values?
   c. Is it good or bad?
   d. Should I believe in it?
   e. None of the above are sociological questions.

d (page 529)

5. Since religions are a major source of norms and values, sociologists understand them to be
   a. among the most important institutions in society.
   b. a significant source of social solidarity.
   c. a frequent source of conflict.
   d. All of the above
   e. None of the above

c (page 530)

6. Sociologists explain the appeal of religion in terms of
   a. the supernatural intervention of spirits or gods.
   b. the psychological experience of the person who is attracted to it.
   c. problems of the social order that threaten a person's sense of well-being.
   d. All of the above
   e. None of the above

e (page 532)

7. What is unique about the New Age religious movement?
   a. its exclusive basis in medieval Christianity
   b. its practice of human sacrifice
   c. its rigid dogmatism
   d. its narrow, inflexible organizational structure
   e. its eclectic openness to diverse practices and beliefs from all over the globe

d (pages 530–531)

8. Which of the following sociological theorists believed that religion would become less and less significant in modern times?
   a. Karl Marx
   b. Émile Durkheim
   c. Max Weber
   d. All of the above
   e. None of the above

b (page 531)

9. Who called religion the "opium of the people"?
   a. Émile Durkheim
   b. Karl Marx
   c. Max Weber
   d. Jesus Christ
   e. Ludwig Feuerbach

a (page 530)

10. Religion is a form of _____, according to Karl Marx, diverting attention from inequalities and injustice and encouraging acceptance of oppression.
    a. alienation
    b. magic
    c. enlightenment
    d. salvation
    e. science

d (page 531)

11. Religion, according to Émile Durkheim, is based on a distinction between the _____ and the _____.
    a. people; natural world
    b. society; natural world
    c. good; bad
    d. sacred; profane
    e. pure; nasty

a (page 531)

12. In Émile Durkheim's terms, objects that are venerated and treated as separate from the routine, everyday aspects of day-to-day existence are
    a. sacred.
    b. profane.
    c. shamans.
    d. magic.
    e. alienated.

d (page 531)

13. Émile Durkheim's theory of religion, which connected it with the overall nature of the institutions of a society, is an example of the _____ tradition.
    a. monotheistic
    b. polytheistic
    c. Marxist
    d. functionalist
    e. symbolic interactionist

b (page 531)

14. What is the social function of religion, according to Émile Durkheim?
    a. It provides justification for those who are in power.
    b. It aids in cohering or providing solidarity by ensuring that people meet regularly to affirm common beliefs and values.
    c. It contributes to the process of social transformation.
    d. All of the above
    e. None of the above

c (page 531)   15. Which of the following saw religion as a potential source
                     of social transformation?
                     a.   Émile Durkheim
                     b.   Karl Marx
                     c.   Max Weber
                     d.   Vladimir Lenin
                     e.   Friedrich Nietzsche

c (page 531)   16. Max Weber saw _____ as the source of the capitalistic
                     outlook found in the modern West.
                     a.   the profit motive
                     b.   money
                     c.   Protestantism
                     d.   Catholicism
                     e.   Islam

e (page 531)   17. Which of the following theorists was most interested in the
                     world's religions?
                     a.   Émile Durkheim
                     b.   Karl Marx
                     c.   Auguste Comte
                     d.   Ludwig Feuerbach
                     e.   Max Weber

c (page 534)   18. Durkheim failed to anticipate the role of religion in
                     a.   promoting social cohesion.
                     b.   enhancing social solidarity.
                     c.   division, conflict, and change in society.
                     d.   its most elementary forms, such as totemism.
                     e.   distinguishing between the sacred and the profane.

a (page 534)   19. A limitation on the applicability of the classic theories of
                     religion (proposed by Marx, Durkheim, and Weber) is
                     a.   their basis in societies in which a single religion
                          prevailed.
                     b.   their basis in outdated religions.
                     c.   their focus on only theistic religions.
                     d.   their refusal to consider how closely religion can be
                          linked with society.
                     e.   their belief that religious values were contrary to those
                          of the larger society.

e (page 535)

20. A rise in worldly thinking coupled with a decline in the influence of religion is called
    a. globalization.
    b. religious pluralism.
    c. new age religion.
    d. theism.
    e. secularization.

d (pages 535)

21. To assess the extent of secularization, sociologists examine
    a. the level of membership in religious organizations.
    b. trends in the amount of social influence, wealth, and prestige held by religious organizations.
    c. the amount of religiosity among the population.
    d. All of the above
    e. None of the above

b (page 536)

22. According to the religious economy approach,
    a. there is only so much religion to go around, so it should be "spent" wisely.
    b. religions can be understood as organizations in competition with one another for followers.
    c. the economy has replaced religion as the major source of values and norms in modern societies.
    d. economic activities are increasingly guided by religious values.
    e. money is the root of all evil.

c (page 536)

23. _____ the classical theorists, religious economists argue that competition with other religious and secular viewpoints _____ religion in society overall.
    a. Unlike; weakens
    b. Like; weakens
    c. Unlike; strengthens
    d. Like; strengthens
    e. Unlike; destroys

d (page 536)

24. In a society with a great deal of pluralism in religion, such as the United States, different religious groups use "marketing techniques" to "package an appealing product" to attract "buyers" in a competitive "market." Which approach in the sociology of religion uses this sort of description?
    a. Marxism
    b. Weberians
    c. functionalism
    d. religious economy
    e. Total Quality Inquisition (TQI)

b (page 537)

25. What proportion of American baby boomers are actually engaged in what religious economists might call "spiritual shopping sprees," according to research by Roof (1993)?
    a. 10 percent
    b. one-third
    c. two-thirds
    d. 80 percent
    e. 95 percent

c (page 537)

26. In the classification of religious organizations based on early theories of Weber, Troeltsch, and Niebuhr, _____ were considered to be most established and conventional, while _____ were placed at the opposite end of the continuum.
    a. sects; churches
    b. churches; sects
    c. churches; cults
    d. cults; churches
    e. cults; sects

d (page 537)

27. Since the terms "sect" and "cult" have negative connotations these days, sociologists now prefer to call such groups
    a. churches.
    b. denominations.
    c. new social movements.
    d. new religious movements.
    e. new age religions.

d (page 537)

28. A religious organization which forms by breaking away from an established church, which relies on people joining rather than being born into the group, and which generally rejects or tries to change the surrounding society would be termed a
    a. religious movement.
    b. denomination.
    c. church.
    d. sect.
    e. cult.

b (page 540)

29. _____ that survive over time become institutionalized as _____.
    a. Churches; sects
    b. Sects; denominations
    c. Denominations; cults
    d. Denominations; churches
    e. Sects; cults

e (page 540)

30. _____ are a form of religious revival, while _____ are a form of religious innovation.
    a. Churches; sects
    b. Sects; denominations
    c. Denominations; cults
    d. Denominations; churches
    e. Sects; cults

a (page 540)

31. An association of people who join together to spread a new religion or a new interpretation of an existing religion is a
    a. religious movement.
    b. denomination.
    c. church.
    d. sect.
    e. cult.

d (page 541)

32. According to Max Weber's theory, leaders who are charismatic
    a. have inspirational qualities capable of capturing the imagination and devotion of a mass of followers.
    b. are usually the main force behind a religious movement in its early phase.
    c. may be political or religious leaders.
    d. All of the above
    e. None of the above

c (page 541)

33. When the leader of a religious movement dies, the movement must
    a. engage in the "routinization of charisma."
    b. fade away.
    c. Either *a* or *b*
    d. Both *a* and *b*
    e. Neither *a* nor *b*

d (page 542)

34. Which of the following would be included in the term "new religious movements"?
    a. the Unification Church
    b. International Society for Krishna Consciousness
    c. New Age self-help seminars
    d. All of the above
    e. None of the above

b (page 543)

35. Which type of new religious movement is most likely to require significant lifestyle changes of its members?
    a. world-affirming movements
    b. world-rejecting movements
    c. world-accommodating movements
    d. world-class movements
    e. world-shattering movements

c (page 543)

36. _____ is the process by which people in society become more concerned with worldly rather than spiritual matters and religious organizations lose their influence over social life.
    a. Charisma
    b. Millenarianism
    c. Secularization
    d. Profanity
    e. Shamanism

a (page 544)

37. _____ other institutions, women have been _____ positions of power in most churches and denominations.
    a. As is the case in; excluded from
    b. As is the case in; incorporated in
    c. Contrary to the situation in; excluded from
    d. Contrary to the situation in; incorporated in
    e. None of the above; women's situation varies greatly from one group to another.

d (page 548)

38. Belief in a single all-knowing, all-powerful god is called
    a. totemism.
    b. animism.
    c. shamanism.
    d. monotheism.
    e. polytheism.

a (page 548)

39. The largest religion in the world, with 2.6 billion followers, is
    a. Christianity.
    b. Islam.
    c. Judaism.
    d. Hinduism.
    e. Buddhism.

b (page 548)

40. The second largest and fastest-growing religion in the world is
    a. Christianity.
    b. Islam.
    c. Judaism.
    d. Hinduism.
    e. Buddhism.

c (page 549)

41. The original source of the world's two largest religions is
    a. Christianity.
    b. Islam.
    c. Judaism.
    d. Hinduism.
    e. Buddhism.

e (page 550)

42. Belief that many gods represent various natural forces is
    a. totemism.
    b. animism.
    c. shamanism.
    d. monotheism.
    e. polytheism.

d (page 550)

43. Which major world religion contains elements of polytheism?
    a. Christianity
    b. Islam
    c. Judaism
    d. Hinduism
    e. Buddhism

e (page 550)

44. According to Lipset, "the most God-believing and religion-adhering, fundamentalist, and religiously traditional country in Christendom" is
    a. Afghanistan.
    b. Great Britain.
    c. Canada.
    d. Italy.
    e. the United States.

d (page 550)

45. Sociologists argue that the United States has a set of religious beliefs through which it interprets its own history in light of some conception of ultimate reality. Bellah refers to this as a(n)
    a. ecclesia.
    b. theism.
    c. nontheistic religion.
    d. civil religion.
    e. historicism.

b (pages 552–553)

46. Since the 1960s, liberal Protestant denominations have _____ in membership, while membership in conservative Protestant denominations has _____.
    a. declined; stayed even
    b. declined; exploded
    c. stayed even; exploded
    d. risen; declined
    e. exploded; declined

a (page 552)

47. Which of the following groups has seen a big decrease in attendance at religious services since the 1960s, largely because of the stance of the organization on birth control?
    a. Catholics
    b. Protestants
    c. Judaism
    d. the new cults
    e. fundamentalists

a (page 557)

48. _____ are those who believe in spiritual salvation through acceptance of Christ; literal interpretation of the Bible; highly emotional, personal spiritual piety; and commitment to spreading "the Word." Of those, _____ are antimodern in many of their beliefs and advocate strict codes of morality and conduct.
   a. Evangelicals; fundamentalists
   b. Liberal Protestants; televangelists
   c. Catholics; Protestants
   d. Fundamentalists; evangelicals
   e. Protestants; Catholics

True/False Questions

F (pages 528–529)

1. Belief in God is the central element of religion, according to the sociological definition.

F (page 537)

2. The most loosely knit and transient of religious organizations are churches.

T (page 536)

3. A society can have high levels of religiosity even if people do not belong to religious organizations or participate in religious rituals in large numbers.

T (page 540)

4. Most of the approximately 100,000 religions humans have developed were initially considered cults by the religious establishment of their times.

T (page 544)

5. In both Buddhism and Christianity, the image of women in sacred texts is less powerful than those of men.

T (page 544)

6. Women can express strong religious beliefs by becoming nuns in both Christianity and Buddhism.

T (page 548)

7. The status of Christianity as the world's largest religion is in part a result of conquest.

F (page 559)

8. Religious nationalism is pluralistic in calling for all religions to embrace the cause of the nation.

F (page 561)   9. Islamic fundamentalism is entirely an outcome of features of the Islamic religion, and has nothing to do with the impact of Western culture on the Muslim world.

Essay Questions

1. The most influential founders of sociology believed that religion would decline in influence as the modern era progressed. This chapter shows that this has not necessarily happened. Explain why.

2. When sociologists study religion, they are not concerned with proving or disproving any particular belief system. What are they concerned with, and how do they study religion?

3. Discuss the rise of New Age religions since the 1960s. What kind of phenomenon is this? How has it been influenced by globalization?

4. Marx argued that religion was a form of self-alienation, and was used to divert attention and thus help maintain inequality and injustice in the world. How do developments in religion in recent decades support and/or contradict his position? Refer to developments such as the rise of Christian televangelism and conservative fundamentalism, growing religious nationalism in parts of the world, and the challenge of Islamic fundamentalism.

5. Summarize the secularization debate. Which position seems most convincing to you? Why?

6. Apply the religious economy approach to the televangelist phenomenon.

7. Have you ever known anyone who (or have you yourself ever) participated in a religious practice or organization considered "weird" by most people in your society? Using the classifications discussed in this chapter, identify what type of organization it was. Justify your analysis.

8. Discuss the historical role of women in religious organizations. How is women's status in other social institutions related to their status in religion? Be sure to base your essay on specific historical references.

9. Explain how Christianity and Islam became the two dominant religions in the world today. Discuss both their specific systems of belief and the historical processes of globalization in your argument.

10. How have you been affected by the revitalization of religion in the United States? How has globalization affected that process?

CHAPTER 18

The Sociology of the Body:
Health and Illness and Sexuality

Multiple-Choice Questions

b (page 569)

1. Eating disorders like anorexia are diseases of
   a. scarcity.
   b. the affluent.
   c. the poor.
   d. the Third World.
   e. the past.

d (page 569)

2. Anorexia and other eating disorders have their origins in
   a. the increasing scarcity of food.
   b. the larger body type of the modern human.
   c. the religious practices of certain orders of nuns.
   d. the changing body image of women in modern societies.
   e. the declining power of men in modern societies.

c (page 570)

3. Why is the topic of eating disorders a good opportunity to apply the sociological imagination?
   a. It is purely a personal trouble.
   b. It is purely a public issue.
   c. It is a case where what appears to be a personal trouble is part of a larger, public issue.
   d. It is simply a product of people's imaginations and doesn't exist as a problem at all.
   e. None of the above; anorexia has nothing to do with the sociological imagination.

a (page 571)

4. The field that studies the ways in which our bodies are affected by social influences is known as
   a. sociology of the body.
   b. social technologies.
   c. physiology.
   d. anatomy.
   e. psychology.

b (page 571)

5. Michel Foucault's term _____ refers to the ways that the body is increasingly something we are compelled to "create" rather than simply accept.
   a. "sociology of the body"
   b. "social technologies"
   c. "physiology"
   d. "anatomy"
   e. "psychology"

a (page 571)

6. Phenomena that used to be natural processes are increasingly socially controlled. Sociologists refer to this transformation as
   a. the socialization of nature.
   b. social technologies.
   c. the naturalization of society.
   d. role theory.
   e. control theory.

b (page 575)

7. Patterns of behavior a sick person adopts in order to minimize the disruptive impact of illness are called
   a. anorexia.
   b. the sick role.
   c. regimes of health.
   d. the health role.
   e. stigma.

d (page 577)

8. To maintain their regimes of health, chronically ill people engage in
   a. illness work.
   b. everyday work.
   c. biographical work.
   d. All of the above
   e. None of the above

c (page 577)

9. According to symbolic interactionists, chronically ill people _____, building or reconstructing their personal narratives to incorporate their illness as part of their lives.
   a. adopt the sick role
   b. do illness work
   c. do biographical work
   d. perform health maintenance
   e. adopt the stigma role

c (page 577)

10. The main institution dealing with sickness in premodern societies was the
    a. hospital.
    b. doctor.
    c. family.
    d. government.
    e. health maintenance organization.

b (page 578)

11. What was the major feature of the development of modern health care systems?
    a. centering the treatment of serious illnesses in the home and family
    b. the application of science to medical diagnosis and cure
    c. a philosophy that focuses on the balance of psychological and physical aspects of the person, with herbal remedies for imbalances
    d. All of the above
    e. None of the above

a (page 578)

12. Which of the following was a characteristic of health in medieval times?
    a. The major illnesses were infectious diseases like tuberculosis and cholera.
    b. The highest rates of death were among the elderly.
    c. Epidemics such as the plague were localized and had a minor impact on the population of Europe.
    d. All of the above
    e. None of the above

b (pages 578–579)

13. Nowadays, a person with an illness may seek assistance from *both* a medical doctor and a homeopath. This is why some sociologists call nonorthodox techniques
    a. alternative medicine.
    b. complementary medicine.
    c. illness work.
    d. the conditional sick role.
    e. the illegitimate role.

a (page 579)   14. Conditions for which most people seek alternative medical treatment are often the result of
        a.   modern life.
        b.   stigmas.
        c.   the regimes of health.
        d.   the sick role.
        e.   bulimia.

c (page 580)   15. The notion that the power of modern medicine will continue to show improvements in public health indefinitely is unsatisfactory to sociologists because
        a.   it is not based in fact.
        b.   the achievements have more to do with luck than science.
        c.   it ignores social and environmental factors in patterns of health and illness.
        d.   All of the above
        e.   None of the above

a (page 582)   16. Which group has the highest life expectancy at birth?
        a.   white females
        b.   white males
        c.   black females
        d.   black males
        e.   None of the above; life expectancy does not vary by sex or race.

c (page 582)   17. Which group had the higher mortality rate due to murder in the 1980s?
        a.   white women over sixty-five
        b.   white men over sixty-five
        c.   black men between fourteen and seventeen
        d.   white men between fourteen and seventeen
        e.   all women between twenty and twenty-four

d (page 582)   18. What would be the most effective policy to counter the effect of poverty on health?
        a.   health education
        b.   disease prevention
        c.   increased access to health care
        d.   reduce or eliminate poverty
        e.   None of the above would have a significant effect on health.

d (pages 582–583) 19. Why did the gender gap in life expectancy increase during the twentieth century?
  a. The major causes of death changed to those influenced by behavior, and women tend to engage in those life-shortening behaviors less than men.
  b. The male gender role contributes to hypertension and heart attacks.
  c. Females have a genetic advantage in their lower incidence of congenital abnormalities.
  d. All of the above
  e. None of the above

a (page 583) 20. Women have _____ on average; they also report _____ more often.
  a. longer lives; poorer health
  b. shorter lives; poorer health
  c. longer lives; better health
  d. shorter lives; better health
  e. None of the above; the differences between men and women are insignificant.

d (page 583) 21. Why do women report poorer health in spite of their longer life expectancies?
  a. Longer life and aging bring more health problems.
  b. Women are more likely to seek medical care.
  c. Women are more likely to use preventive health care services.
  d. All of the above
  e. None of the above

c (pages 580–582) 22. Why is education correlated with inequalities in health and illness?
  a. Poor children are more likely to be exposed to asbestos in schools.
  b. People with higher levels of education are more likely to have friends who are doctors.
  c. People with higher levels of education are more likely to exercise and less likely to smoke or be overweight.
  d. All of the above
  e. None of the above

a (page 580)

23. Why do differences in occupational status lead to inequalities in health and illness?
    a. Those who work in offices are at less risk of injury or exposure to hazardous materials.
    b. White-collar workers have more stressful jobs than blue-collar workers.
    c. In all societies, white-collar workers have better access to health care than blue-collar workers.
    d. All of the above
    e. None of the above

c (page 584)

24. According to Richard Wilkinson, the healthiest societies in the world are those with the most
    a. wealth.
    b. income.
    c. egalitarian distribution of income.
    d. unequal distribution of income.
    e. unequal distribution of wealth.

a (page 585)

25. Which of the following was an effect of colonialism on health?
    a. Entire native populations in the Americas were wiped out due to exposure to diseases like smallpox, to which they had no resistance.
    b. The plague (the "Black Death") was introduced to Europe from Africa.
    c. Nutrition for colonized peoples improved, which had a positive impact on their health.
    d. All of the above
    e. None of the above

b (page 585)

26. The impact of colonialism on people's nutritional health was that
    a. the nutrition of the colonized people improved while the nutrition of the colonizers deteriorated.
    b. the nutrition of the colonized people suffered while the nutrition of the colonizers improved.
    c. the nutrition of both the colonized people and the colonizers improved.
    d. the nutrition of both the colonized people and the colonizers suffered.
    e. None of the above; there was no impact.

e (page 587)   27. How many sexual identities were identified by Judith Lorber (1994)?

     a. only one; all humans have essential the same sexual identity

     b. only two—male and female

     c. three—male, female, and gay

     d. four—male, female, lesbian, and gay

     e. ten

c (page 587)   28. Which was considered the highest form of sexual love by the ancient Greeks?

     a. the love of a man for his wife

     b. the love of a man for his mistress

     c. the love of men for boys

     d. All of the above were equally valued by the ancient Greeks.

     e. None of the above were tolerated by the ancient Greeks.

b (page 587)   29. How do we know that sexual responses are learned, rather than inborn?

     a. All humans practice essentially the same sexual behaviors.

     b. There is tremendous variation in what different cultures consider "natural" sexual behavior.

     c. All cultures practice extended foreplay, which is learned behavior.

     d. All of the above

     e. None of the above; sexual response is innate, not learned.

d (page 588)   30. For most of the past two thousand years in the West,

     a. attitudes toward sexuality were shaped by Christianity.

     b. the dominant view was that sexual behavior, except for reproduction, was suspect.

     c. the idea that sexual fulfillment is a goal of marriage was rare.

     d. All of the above

     e. None of the above

b (page 589)

31. In Victorian times, men who visited prostitutes or kept mistresses were accepted in polite society, but women who engaged in similar behavior were shunned. This _____ persists in some ways even today.
    a. single standard
    b. double standard
    c. universal stigma
    d. double stigma
    e. polymorphous perversity

d (page 590)

32. Alfred Kinsey's study of the sexual behavior of white Americans in the 1940s and 1950s found
    a. significant differences between public standards and private practices.
    b. evidence of the double standard toward male and female sexuality.
    c. a majority of both men and women had engaged in masturbation and oral sex.
    d. All of the above
    e. None of the above

c (page 590)

33. What was the most significant finding of Lillian Rubin's study of sexuality among Americans in the late 1980s?
    a. Men reported difficulty finding available female sexual partners, leading to widespread male sexual frustration.
    b. Women were even less interested in their own sexual satisfaction than they were in Kinsey's 1940 study.
    c. Women expect to receive as well as provide sexual satisfaction, leading many men to feel "inadequate."
    d. All of the above
    e. None of the above

c (page 591)

34. What conclusion can be drawn from both Lillian Rubin's and Edward Laumann et al.'s recent research on sexuality in America?
    a. Sexual behavior is generally more liberal than most people would have thought.
    b. Very little has really changed since Kinsey's research in the 1940s and 1950s.
    c. Young people are more sexually active before marriage than was true in the past.
    d. All of the above
    e. None of the above

d (page 591)

35. Higher rates of sexual activity among teens are associated with
    a. lower socioeconomic status.
    b. lower school performance.
    c. high levels of "body pride."
    d. All of the above
    e. None of the above

d (page 591)

36. One probable reason for the differences between Kinsey's and Laumann's findings on sexual behavior in the United States is
    a. that Americans have become much more sexually conservative since the 1940s.
    b. Kinsey's team lied about their findings.
    c. Laumann's team lied about their findings.
    d. their methods—specifically their samples—were quite different.
    e. None of the above accounts for the discrepancies.

a (page 594)

37. _____ is the direction of one's sexual or romantic attraction.
    a. Sexual orientation
    b. Sexual preference
    c. Sexism
    d. Romanticism
    e. Sex role

b (page 594)

38. _____ is a misleading term because it implies such attractions are entirely a matter of personal choice.
    a. Sexual orientation
    b. Sexual preference
    c. Sexism
    d. Romanticism
    e. Sex role

c (page 594)

39. The most commonly found sexual orientation in all cultures is
    a. homosexuality.
    b. lesbianism.
    c. heterosexuality.
    d. bisexuality.
    e. asexuality.

e (page 594)

40. People who experience sexual or romantic attraction for persons of either sex are referred to as
    a. heterosexuals.
    b. homosexuals.
    c. lesbians.
    d. gays.
    e. bisexuals.

d (page 594)

41. Ritualized male-male sexual encounters were found to have been the norm in
    a. ancient Greece among highly educated men and boys.
    b. nineteenth century Japan among heterosexual samurai warriors.
    c. several tribes in Melanesia and New Guinea.
    d. All of the above
    e. None of the above; such behavior has never been the norm.

d (page 595)

42. Biological explanations for homosexuality have focused on
    a. brain characteristics.
    b. effects on fetal development of the mother's in-utero hormone production.
    c. only small numbers of cases.
    d. All of the above
    e. None of the above

d (page 595)

43. Twin studies by Bailey and Pillard suggest that homosexuality is a result of
    a. personal choice.
    b. biological factors.
    c. social learning.
    d. a complex interplay between *b* and *c*.
    e. None of the above

b (page 595)

44. Aversion to or hatred of homosexuals and their lifestyles and behavior based on such feelings is termed
    a. sexism.
    b. homophobia.
    c. heterophobia.
    d. biphobia.
    e. DSM.

c (page 596)   45. What proportion of Americans believe homosexuality is
                        "morally wrong"?
                        a.   6 percent
                        b.   two-fifths
                        c.   three-fifths
                        d.   75 percent
                        e.   nine-tenths

b (page 596)   46. The current global wave of gay and lesbian civil rights
                        movements initially grew out of
                        a.   movements to legalize marijuana in Amsterdam.
                        b.   1960s social movements in the United States.
                        c.   the pro-life movement.
                        d.   the Islamic revolution in Iran.
                        e.   liberation theology.

d (pages 597–598)   47. Which of the following is an example of procreative
                        technology?
                        a.   contraception
                        b.   the medicalization of pregnancy and childbirth
                        c.   genetic engineering
                        d.   All of the above
                        e.   None of the above

d (pages 597–598)   48. Which of the following is an example of the socialization
                        of nature?
                        a.   contraception
                        b.   the medicalization of pregnancy and childbirth
                        c.   genetic engineering
                        d.   All of the above
                        e.   None of the above

a (page 598)   49. Sociologists are concerned that unequal access to genetic
                        engineering because of its cost could lead to
                        a.   a "biological underclass."
                        b.   a "master race."
                        c.   genetic dilution of existing pure races.
                        d.   All of the above
                        e.   None of the above

b (page 598)

50. Genetic engineering is perhaps the ultimate expression of
    a. man's inhumanity.
    b. the socialization of nature.
    c. the naturalization of society.
    d. sexual disorientation.
    e. None of the above

a (page 598)

51. What belief do both sides of the abortion debate have in common, which is the source of a potential constructive dialogue, according to Ronald Dworkin?
    a. belief in the sanctity of human life (the child's on one side, the mother's on the other)
    b. belief in the rights of the unborn
    c. belief in the rights of women
    d. All of the above
    e. None of the above

True/False Questions

F (page 570)

1. Anorexia was first identified as a disorder in Somalia in 1984.

T (page 570)

2. As many as 85 percent of American college women have serious problems with eating disorders at some point in their college careers.

T (page 570)

3. It is the abundance of food, not its scarcity, that leads to the increase in eating disorders like anorexia.

T (page 580)

4. Effective sanitation, better nutrition, control of sewage, and improved hygiene were more important than medicine in the decline of death rates prior to the twentieth century.

F (page 580)

5. The fact that lower classes in industrialized countries have worse health and higher mortality rates is the simple result of lower income.

F (page 582)

6. The health differences between whites and blacks in the United States can be attributed entirely to the differences in social class between the two groups.

T (page 585)   7. Before the Europeans came, the native peoples of the Americas did not suffer from infectious diseases to the extent the Europeans did.

T (page 585)   8. Much disease in the Third World is due to a lack of the most basic of services: clean, safe water and sanitary treatment of sewage.

F (page 594)   9. Unlike other human behaviors, it is clear that sexuality is genetically determined.

T (page 594)   10. Homosexuality exists in all cultures.

Essay Questions

1. Why is anorexia found predominantly among young women? Why has its incidence been increasing over the past thirty or forty years? Why is it spreading globally?

2. Why is it necessary to have a sociology of the body as we move into the twenty-first century?

3. Describe and discuss the implications of three examples of *social technologies.* Consider the impact on yourself and society as a whole.

4. Outline Talcott Parsons's concept of the sick role. Be sure to discuss the three "pillars" of the sick role, as well as the three versions it might take. How does this concept fit with functionalist assumptions?

5. How do symbolic interactionists approach the study of illness and health? What is meant by "regimes of health," and what forms of "work" are involved?

6. Why are people increasingly seeking treatments for their conditions from various forms of alternative medicine? In what ways are they dissatisfied with conventional medicine? Why does conventional medicine not seem to have answers for some of these conditions?

7. Describe the unequal distribution of health based on race, gender, and class.

8. One of the justifications for colonialism was the supposed benefits of civilization for the indigenous peoples in the conquered lands. What were the actual impacts, particularly in terms of health and disease?

9. Explain this statement in the text: "The global AIDS epidemic and attempts to halt its spread are further examples of the socialization of nature."

10. Discuss current research on the interplay of biology and social learning in shaping sexual behavior, and sexual orientation in particular.

CHAPTER 19

Urbanization, Population, and the Environment

Multiple-Choice Questions

d (page 603)   1. New York City has become what urban sociologists refer to as a
    a. suburban sprawl.
    b. developing nation.
    c. population pyramid.
    d. tourist city.
    e. primary group.

e (page 604)   2. In modern societies, most of the population lives
    a. on small, isolated farms.
    b. in the countryside.
    c. in villages.
    d. in small towns.
    e. in cities.

d (page 605)   3. Where did the first cities emerge about 3,500 B.C.E.?
    a. the Nile River valley
    b. the valley of the Tigris and Euphrates rivers
    c. the Indus River valley
    d. All of the above
    e. None of the above

a (page 605)   4. In most ancient cities,
    a. an outer wall offered both military defense and separation from the countryside.
    b. the central area was primarily a business district, much like cities today.
    c. the elite lived on the perimeter, or even outside the walls.
    d. All of the above
    e. None of the above

a (page 605)

5. A cluster of cities and towns forming a continuous network is called a(n)
   a. conurbation.
   b. metropolis.
   c. megalomaniac.
   d. urbanization.
   e. gentrification.

c (page 605)

6. A term originally referring to an ancient Greek utopian planned city-state, but now applied to a "city of cities" is
   a. mega-urbation.
   b. metropolis.
   c. megalopolis.
   d. urbanization.
   e. gentrification.

d (page 605)

7. Industrialization generated _____, the movement of population from the countryside into towns and cities.
   a. conurbation
   b. metropolization
   c. megalomania
   d. urbanization
   e. gentrification

d (page 606)

8. Urbanization in the twenty-first century is a _____ process.
   a. First World
   b. Second World
   c. Third World
   d. global
   e. localized

a (page 607)

9. Cities, like plant and animal populations, grow following principles of adaptation and equilibrium, so that neighborhoods are settled in a process of competition, invasion, and competition. This is the idea behind
   a. urban ecology or the ecological approach to urban analysis.
   b. urbanism as a way of life.
   c. the created environment approach to urban analysis.
   d. collective consumption.
   e. collective conscience.

b (page 606)

10. Louis Wirth saw _____ as an approach that explains how the cultural life of cities comes to dominate areas outside cities as well.
    a. urban ecology, or the ecological approach to urban analysis,
    b. urbanism as a way of life
    c. the created environment approach to urban analysis
    d. collective consumption
    e. collective conscience

a (page 608)

11. Louis Wirth's idea that _____ characterizes modern cities was an overgeneralization.
    a. impersonality
    b. intimacy
    c. diversity
    d. All of the above
    e. None of the above

d (page 609)

12. Jane Jacobs's idea that the large number of "respectable eyes" on the streets of a large city would keep behavior under control failed to take into account _____ in modern cities.
    a. economic inequalities
    b. cultural differences
    c. extremes of behavior
    d. All of the above
    e. None of the above

c (page 610)

13. According to David Harvey, industrial capitalism continually restructures space in its pursuit of profits. This theoretical approach is known as
    a. urban ecology or the ecological approach to urban analysis.
    b. urbanism as a way of life.
    c. the created environment approach to urban analysis.
    d. collective consumption.
    e. collective conscience.

d (page 611)

14. Manuel Castells emphasized the struggles of underprivileged groups participating in the process of _____ as an important factor in urban development.
    a. urban ecology or the ecological approach to urban analysis
    b. urbanism as a way of life
    c. the created environment approach to urban analysis
    d. collective consumption
    e. collective conscience

c (page 612)

15. Both David Harvey and Manuel Castells stressed the _____ of cities.
    a. natural growth
    b. ecological processes
    c. political, economic, and social construction
    d. All of the above
    e. None of the above

a (page 612)

16. The key factors structuring modern city neighborhoods, according to John Logan and Harvey Molotch's research, are
    a. tensions and conflicts between different groups, such as large business and local residents.
    b. ecological processes.
    c. the urban "ways of life."
    d. acts of collective consumption.
    e. acts of collective conscience.

c (page 612)

17. Most contemporary theory and research in urban sociology focuses on cities as
    a. natural formations.
    b. places of conflict.
    c. created environments or social constructions.
    d. danger zones of incivility.
    e. None of the above

a (page 612)

18. The massive development and inhabiting of towns surrounding cities is a process known as
    a. suburbanization.
    b. metropolization.
    c. megalomania.
    d. urbanization.
    e. gentrification.

c (page 612)

19. The rapid increase in suburbanization in the United States occurred in the
    a. 1920s.
    b. 1930s and 1940s.
    c. 1950s and 1960s.
    d. 1980s.
    e. 1990s.

d (pages 612–613)

20. What made suburbanization possible in the United States?
    a. the "American dream"—owning a house and some land
    b. Federal Housing Assistance (FHA) loans
    c. the massive highways program of the Eisenhower administration
    d. All of the above
    e. None of the above

d (page 613)

21. Why have the inner-cities in the United States decayed in the last fifty years?
    a. Businesses, jobs, and middle-class residents have moved to the suburbs.
    b. Manufacturing industries have been disappeared, taking away many of the blue-collar jobs for which lower-class residents were qualified.
    c. Segregation has contributed to the social isolation of the "ghetto poor," causing an increase in social problems.
    d. All of the above
    e. None of the above

e (page 617)

22. When more affluent groups move back into cities and renovate dilapidated buildings and neighborhoods, the process is called
    a. conurbation.
    b. metropolization.
    c. megalomania.
    d. urbanization.
    e. gentrification.

b (page 619)

23. The coordination of global business activity takes place in _____ like New York and Tokyo.
    a. conurbations
    b. global cities
    c. megalomania
    d. urban ghettos
    e. suburban zones

e (page 619)

24. Far from disappearing or becoming irrelevant, large
_____ are the hubs of the global economy.
 a. factories
 b. universities
 c. cooperatives
 d. farms
 e. cities

a (page 619)

25. _____ is the term Saskia Sassen uses to refer to urban
centers that host the headquarters of large, transnational
corporations and extensive financial, technological, and
consulting services.
 a. "Global city"
 b. "Megalopolis"
 c. "Transnational capitol"
 d. "Capital hub"
 e. "Megacity"

b (page 619)

26. The global city takes on a geography of "centrality and
marginality," meaning
 a. the globalization process is central, pushing cities to
 the margins of the economy.
 b. the space of the city is increasingly devoted to the
 needs of wealth, and the city is made unliveable for the
 poor.
 c. affluent city dwellers flee the central city for its
 furthest margins.
 d. the poor "untouchables" transform the cityscape to
 serve their needs, rather than those of the affluent.
 e. None of the above

b (page 621)

27. According to Castells, megacities are
 a. not really as large as most cities.
 b. connection points between huge populations of people
 and the global economy.
 c. overwhelmingly populated by people who would be
 considered successful in the global economy.
 d. All of the above
 e. None of the above

d (page 621)   28. Urban growth in less developed regions is high because of
        a. high fertility rates.
        b. high rates of internal migration.
        c. high rates of migration from other countries.
        d. both *a* and *b*
        e. both *a* and *c*

b (page 626)   29. Demography is
        a. the study of natural features of the planet.
        b. the study of population.
        c. the study of representative government.
        d. rule by the people.
        e. the study of liberals.

a (page 626)   30. The _____ is the number of live births per year per thousand of the population.
        a. crude birth rate
        b. fertility
        c. fecundity
        d. crude death rate
        e. rate of population growth or decline

b (page 627)   31. _____ refers to the number of live-born children the average woman has.
        a. Crude birth rate
        b. Fertility
        c. Fecundity
        d. Crude death rate
        e. Rate of population growth or decline

c (page 627)   32. _____ is the potential number of children women are biologically able to bear.
        a. Crude birth rate
        b. Fertility
        c. Fecundity
        d. Crude death rate
        e. Infant mortality rate

d (page 627)   33. The _____ is the number of deaths per thousand of population per year.
        a. crude birth rate
        b. fertility
        c. fecundity
        d. crude death rate
        e. infant mortality rate

e (page 627)

34. The number of babies per thousand of population who die
in any year before reaching one year of age is called the
   a. crude birth rate.
   b. fertility.
   c. fecundity.
   d. crude death rate.
   e. infant mortality rate.

a (page 627)

35. The number of years an average person can expect to live is
called
   a. life expectancy.
   b. fertility.
   c. fecundity.
   d. crude death rate.
   e. life span.

e (page 627)

36. The maximum number of years that an individual could
possibly live is called
   a. life expectancy.
   b. fertility.
   c. fecundity.
   d. crude death rate.
   e. life span.

e (page 627)

37. The _____ is calculated by subtracting the number of
deaths per thousand from the number of births per thousand
in a year.
   a. crude birth rate
   b. fertility
   c. fecundity
   d. crude death rate
   e. rate of population growth or decline

b (page 627)

38. Population growth rates are
   a. linear.
   b. exponential.
   c. usually negative.
   d. All of the above
   e. None of the above

b (page 632)   39. The period of time it takes the population to double is
                    known as the
                    a. crude birth rate.
                    b. doubling time.
                    c. secundity.
                    d. crude death rate.
                    e. rate of population growth or decline.

a (page 632)   40. _____ refers to the belief that population growth tends
                    to outstrip expansion of food production, leading to natural
                    curbs on population like famine and war.
                    a. Malthusianism
                    b. Demographic transition
                    c. Fertility
                    d. Fecundity
                    e. Faminism

b (page 632)   41. According to demographic transition theory, in which stage
                    does high population growth take place?
                    a. Stage 1 (pre-industrial, traditional)
                    b. Stage 2 (partial industrialization)
                    c. Stage 3 (full industrialization)
                    d. Stage 4 (post-industrial)
                    e. Stage 5 (cosmic exploration)

b (page 632)   42. _____ refers to the theory that economic development
                    generated by industrialization leads to population stability.
                    a. Malthusianism
                    b. Demographic transition
                    c. Fertility
                    d. Fecundity
                    e. Economism

b (page 634)   43. In the United Nations' "medium scenario"—the fertility
                    rate considered most likely to occur—world population
                    will reach _____ in 2150.
                    a. 5.6 billion
                    b. 10.8 billion
                    c. 15 billion
                    d. 25 billion
                    e. None of the above; the UN considers it unlikely any
                       humans will be alive by then.

e (page 634)

44. With global hunger and malnourishment already affecting _____ people today, the problem is likely to _____ .
   a.   20 million; diminish
   b.   100 million; finally disappear by 2050
   c.   260 million; diminish significantly in the next twenty years
   d.   500 million; get worse
   e.   830 million; get worse

a (page 637)

45. When the buildup of carbon dioxide in the atmosphere acts like the glass on a greenhouse and causes the average temperature of the earth to rise, the process is called
   a.   global warming.
   b.   depletion of the ozone layer.
   c.   toxic waste.
   d.   recycling.
   e.   the Greenpeace effect.

b (page 637)

46. Gases previously used in aerosols and refrigerants have caused
   a.   global warming.
   b.   depletion of the ozone layer.
   c.   toxic waste.
   d.   recycling.
   e.   the Greenpeace effect.

c (page 638)

47. The origins of the substantial human impact on the environment are
   a.   natural.
   b.   biological.
   c.   social.
   d.   All of the above
   e.   None of the above

d (pages 638–639)

48. The solution to the environmental crises will require
   a.   social changes.
   b.   technological changes.
   c.   global cooperation.
   d.   All of the above
   e.   None of the above

c (pages 614–615)   49. Why have jobs shifted from manufacturing to service and from the Northeast to the South and West?
　　a.　This is the natural evolution of the economy.
　　b.　The jobs are simply following the population shift—more people are migrating to those regions.
　　c.　Globalization and the mobility of capital allow firms to seek areas where labor costs are lower due to weaker unions and bigger tax breaks.
　　d.　All of the above
　　e.　None of the above

b (page 637)   50. The Brundtland Commission coined the term _____, which means "meeting the needs of the present, without compromising the ability of future generations to meet their own needs."
　　a.　"development"
　　b.　"sustainable development"
　　c.　"modernization"
　　d.　"postmodernization"
　　e.　"knowledge economy"

True/False Questions

F (page 604)   1. Accounts of city life in the late nineteenth and early twentieth centuries were universally optimistic.

T (page 606)   2. The first major sociological theories of urban life were developed at the University of Chicago, hence the name "Chicago School."

T (page 607)   3. Urban ecology failed to account for processes of social construction, such as racial discrimination and segregation, in the development of cities.

T (page 613)   4. Federal programs funded almost half the suburban housing built in the U.S. during the 1950s and 1960s.

T (page 613)   5. The minority populations of suburbs are now growing faster than that of whites.

F (page 618)   6. Elijah Anderson found that gentrification generally improved conditions for the neighborhood's poorer residents.

F (page 619)   7. Cities as we know them are rapidly being rendered irrelevant by cyberspace and the global economy.

T (page 627)   8. The infant mortality rate has a significant influence on life expectancy.

F (page 634)   9. China's population control policy has failed to control the rapid growth of its population.

T (page 638)   10. The known energy resources are not sufficient for the Third World to attain a level of energy consumption comparable to that of the First World.

Essay Questions

1. As noted in the introductory section of this chapter, sociologists ask two general questions about city life: "Is social life in cities distinctive from social life outside of cities?" and "How much is urban life influenced by larger social forces?" Based on your reading of the chapter, how would you respond to these two questions?

2. Describe city life in traditional societies. What are the biggest differences between cities then and cities now?

3. Discuss the approaches to understanding urbanism developed by the Chicago School. How have contributions by new researchers, such as Jane Jacobs, David Harvey, and Manuel Castells added to or replaced the earlier views of Park, Burgess, and Wirth?

4. Describe the process of suburbanization as it has occurred in the United States. How has it contributed to urban problems? What other processes have been involved in those problems?

5. How is globalization affecting the largest cities in the world? Outline Sassen's concept of the "global city." What are the four key traits of these urban centers?

6. Mike Davis refers to a "conscious 'hardening' of the city surface against the poor." Describe how this process is affecting the city to which he is referring. Is this process occurring on a global scale? Explain.

7. What is causing such rapid growth in the cities of developing countries? What challenges do those cities face in dealing with this tremendous influx?

8. Is Malthusianism irrelevant in the twenty-first century? How does the *demographic transition* explain population trends? Which approach appears to predict the patterns of population growth in the developing world? Will the effects of population growth on the environment have an impact on prospects for economic improvement in the developing world?

9. Why is the environment a sociological issue? What will be required to make the transition from current processes of environmental degradation to sustainable development?

10. What are the prospects for the environment in your lifetime? How will you be affected by such prospects?

CHAPTER 20

Globalization in a Changing World

Multiple-Choice Questions

e (page 643)

1. Hypothetically, if all of human existence had taken place in one day, modern societies would have developed
   a. at about noon.
   b. at 3:00 P.M.
   c. at 7:30 P.M.
   d. at 11:56 P.M.
   e. at 11:59:30 P.M.

a (page 644)

2. Transformation of the social institutions and culture of a society over time is called
   a. social change.
   b. social continuation.
   c. radical change.
   d. evolution.
   e. collective behavior.

d (page 644)

3. Which of the following factors has consistently influenced social change over time?
   a. the physical environment
   b. political organization
   c. cultural factors
   d. All of the above
   e. None of the above

d (page 645)

4. Which of the following is included in the cultural factors that might influence social change?
   a. religion
   b. communication systems
   c. leadership
   d. All of the above
   e. None of the above

b (page 646)

5. What invention first made possible increased control of material resources, the development of large-scale organizations, and an altered sense of past, present, and future?
   a. the wheel
   b. writing
   c. capitalism
   d. the computer
   e. None of the above

a (page 646)

6. Leaders can only be effective in bringing about social change if
   a. favorable social conditions exist as well.
   b. they are charismatic.
   c. they are authoritarian.
   d. All of the above
   e. None of the above

b (page 646)

7. _____ have subsumed the physical environment as a factor in social change over the last two hundred years.
   a. Religions
   b. Economic influences
   c. Political influences
   d. All of the above
   e. None of the above

c (page 646)

8. The most far-reaching economic influence on social change has been
   a. the invention of the wheel.
   b. the invention of the hammer.
   c. the impact of industrial capitalism.
   d. the invention of the sickle.
   e. the impact of the Great Depression.

d (page 646)

9. Capitalism stimulates social change in an unprecedented way because it
   a. involves the constant expansion of production.
   b. involves the ever-increasing accumulation of wealth.
   c. promotes constant revision of the technology of production, increasingly drawing science into the process.
   d. All of the above
   e. None of the above

b (page 647)

10. What was the most significant political factor in speeding up patterns of change in the modern world?
   a. the invention of the ballot box
   b. the emergence of the modern state
   c. the commitment to less government involvement in social life and the economy
   d. All of the above
   e. None of the above

d (page 647)

11. The cultural factors that have most influenced social change, including political change and revolution, include
   a. the development of science.
   b. the secularization of thought.
   c. the critical and innovative character of the modern outlook.
   d. All of the above
   e. None of the above

d (page 648)

12. Which term has been used to describe the new society that is no longer based on industrialism?
   a. "information society"
   b. "service society"
   c. "knowledge society"
   d. All of the above
   e. None of the above

c (page 648)

13. Daniel Bell and Alain Touraine both used the term _____ to refer to the new society that is no longer dependent on industrialism.
   a. "information society"
   b. "service society"
   c. "postindustrial"
   d. All of the above
   e. None of the above

b (page 648)

14. What feature is displacing the manufacture of material goods as the basis of the production system?
   a. the consumption of material goods
   b. information and knowledge
   c. agriculture
   d. hunting
   e. fishing

c (page 648)

15. The most essential type of employee in the postindustrial order, according to Daniel Bell, is the _____ worker.
    a. blue-collar
    b. pink-collar
    c. white-collar
    d. factory
    e. agricultural

a (page 648)

16. Systematic, coordinated information, or _____, is now society's most strategic resource, according to Daniel Bell.
    a. codified knowledge
    b. stratified knowledge
    c. blue-collar work
    d. bureaucracy
    e. None of the above

d (pages 648–649)

17. Which of the following is a valid criticism of Daniel Bell's postindustrial society thesis?
    a. Service occupations are not equal; some involve very little specialized knowledge.
    b. Most service jobs are really part of a larger process that ends in the production of material goods.
    c. Microprocessing and electronic communication technology is being integrated within manufacturing, not replacing it.
    d. All of the above
    e. None of the above

b (page 649)

18. The belief that society is no longer controlled by history and progress is termed
    a. postindustrialism.
    b. postmodernism.
    c. historicity.
    d. posthistoricity.
    e. progressivism.

e (page 649)

19. In the postmodern world, according to postmodernists, there is
    a. great historical progress.
    b. a universal culture worldwide.
    c. great stability.
    d. All of the above
    e. None of the above

b (page 649)

20. According to advocates of postmodernity, the current period is the _____ of history because _____ has triumphed worldwide.
    a. beginning; capitalist democracy
    b. end; capitalist democracy
    c. beginning; communism
    d. end; communism
    e. midpoint; socialism

d (page 649)

21. In the *Risk Society*, according to German sociologist Ulrich Beck, risks are _____, not personal.
    a. global
    b. accidental
    c. a result of natural processes
    d. All of the above
    e. None of the above

b (page 650)

22. Globalization is
    a. the most purely economic stage in human history.
    b. a condition of "one world" interdependence.
    c. rapidly diminishing the amount of human interaction.
    d. All of the above
    e. None of the above

a (page 650)

23. Since the 1960s, the biggest contribution to accelerating and deepening the process of globalization has been made by the rapid development and diffusion of _____ technologies, which have enhanced the "compression" of time and space.
    a. communication
    b. transportation
    c. manufacturing
    d. accounting
    e. energy

e (page 651)

24. According to the text, globalization is being driven by the integration of the world economy, which is now dominated by activity that is
    a. non-economic.
    b. material.
    c. dense.
    d. massive.
    e. weightless.

c (page 652)   25. According to the text, among the most significant political
                    causes of globalization was
                    a.   the development of a socialist alternative to the
                         capitalist world market.
                    b.   the rise of Islamic fundamentalism as a response to
                         Western political influence in the Arab world.
                    c.   the collapse of the Soviet bloc and the end of isolation
                         for the former "Second World."
                    d.   All of the above
                    e.   None of the above

d (page 652)   26. Contributing to the intensification of globalization has been
                    the growing influence of
                    a.   international and regional mechanisms of government.
                    b.   intergovernmental organizations.
                    c.   international non-governmental organizations.
                    d.   All of the above
                    e.   None of the above

d (page 653)   27. According to the text, the global flow of information has
                    resulted in
                    a.   an increased sense that human responsibility for others
                         extends beyond national boundaries.
                    b.   intensification of local cultural identities.
                    c.   intensified allegiance to the nation-state.
                    d.   *a* and *b* only
                    e.   *b* and *c* only

c (page 653)   28. At the heart of economic globalization are the
                    a.   INGOs.
                    b.   IGOs.
                    c.   TNCs.
                    d.   BSEs.
                    e.   TLCs.

a (page 656)   29. Which perspective argues that regionalization within the
                    world economy produces *less* integration and that national
                    governments continue to play a vital role in the economy?
                    a.   the skeptics
                    b.   the hyperglobalizers
                    c.   the transformationalists
                    d.   the "critics"
                    e.   the "hyperventilators"

b (page 657) 30. Which perspective, exemplified by Kenichi Ohmae, argues that globalization is producing a "borderless world" in which national governments are no longer in control of their own economies, resulting in a loss of faith by their citizens?
   a. the skeptics
   b. the hyperglobalizers
   c. the transformationalists
   d. the "critics"
   e. the "hyperventilators"

c (page 657) 31. Which view in the globalization debate takes a "middle position," seeing many old patterns persisting while the broader global order is being transformed, in a dynamic process that is open to influence and change?
   a. the skeptics
   b. the hyperglobalizers
   c. the transformationalists
   d. the "critics"
   e. the "hyperventilators"

c (page 657) 32. Which perspective sees the political structures of countries adapting to challenges from new forms of economic and social organization, from corporations to social movements?
   a. the skeptics
   b. the hyperglobalizers
   c. the transformationalists
   d. the "critics"
   e. the "hyperventilators"

c (page 658) 33. According to the text, a "new individualism" is affecting people in their everyday lives, in which
   a. tradition and custom are re-intensified.
   b. established values are held to be sacred and inviolable.
   c. they must actively construct their own identities in an open and reflexive way.
   d. All of the above
   e. None of the above

d (page 658)   34. In terms of their working lives, globalization makes it more
                     likely that individuals will experience
                     a.   a stable job for life.
                     b.   an exciting career in manufacturing.
                     c.   an exciting career in agriculture.
                     d.   a self-made career path, with several changes over
                          their lifetime.
                     e.   None of the above

d (page 659)   35. Films like *Titanic*
                     a.   invoke ideas that resonate in many different cultures
                          and societies.
                     b.   reflect a shift in values in many societies from old
                          traditions to a more Western view.
                     c.   contribute to a shift in values in many societies from
                          old traditions to a more Western view.
                     d.   All of the above
                     e.   None of the above

b (page 660)   36. Sociologists who see an agenda in the spread of Western-
                     made films and television programs that promotes the
                     political, social, and economic interests of the West call this
                     process
                     a.   hyperglobalization.
                     b.   cultural imperialism.
                     c.   Westernization.
                     d.   differentiation.
                     e.   hybrid identity formation.

d (page 660)   37. Sociologists like Baudrillard and Stuart Hall see the effects
                     of globalization on culture as a process of increasing
                     diversity and fragmentation, or
                     a.   hyperglobalization.
                     b.   cultural imperialism.
                     c.   Westernization.
                     d.   differentiation.
                     e.   the end of history.

b (page 660)   38. As a result of globalization, humans now face risks created
                     by the impact of our own knowledge and technology on the
                     natural world, or
                     a.   external risk.
                     b.   manufactured risk.
                     c.   natural risk.
                     d.   hyper-risk.
                     e.   the end of risk.

a (page 661)

39. According to the text, the interdependence of a globalized world makes environmental risks like global warming more likely, but finding _____ nearly impossible.
    a. the precise causes
    b. the general causes
    c. the consequences
    d. the solutions
    e. the evidence

c (page 661)

40. Depletion of the ozone layer is a manufactured risk that likely contributes to
    a. new forms of "hybrid identity."
    b. mad cow disease.
    c. increased risk of skin cancer.
    d. All of the above
    e. None of the above

c (page 666)

41. The hazards of the risk society, according to Ulrich Beck,
    a. are limited to environmental and health concerns.
    b. affect only those in the most affluent societies.
    c. are not restricted spatially, temporally, or socially.
    d. All of the above
    e. None of the above

a (page 666)

42. Globalization is _____ process; the disparity between the developed and developing world is _____ .
    a. an uneven; greater than ever
    b. a leveling; decreasing rapidly
    c. an uneven; growing, but is still less than it was in the nineteenth century
    d. a leveling; slowly shrinking
    e. None of the above; globalization has little effect on development.

d (page 668)

43. Organizations such as the World Trade Organization argue that liberalized trade regulations and reduced trade barriers will
    a. benefit the developed countries.
    b. benefit the developing nations.
    c. improve integration in the global economy.
    d. All of the above
    e. None of the above

e (page 669)

44. The campaign for "global justice" is
   a. anti-globalization.
   b. in favor of the policies proposed by the World Trade Organization.
   c. opposed to "sustainable development."
   d. All of the above
   e. None of the above

d (page 669)

45. Protestors against the WTO claim it is
   a. undemocratic.
   b. more concerned with corporate profits than human rights.
   c. dominated by the United States.
   d. All of the above
   e. None of the above

True/False Questions

F (page 645)

1. Human beings will always adapt their societies to make the most productive use of their immediate physical environment.

T (page 646)

2. Economic influences are the most important factor driving social change today.

T (page 648)

3. The term first used by Daniel Bell and Alain Touraine to describe societal development beyond the industrial era was "postindustrial society."

T (page 648)

4. Contrary to the theories of postindustrial society, the biggest shift in employment has been from agriculture to all other sectors.

T (page 648)

5. The "postindustrial society" thesis ignores the fact that many service jobs contribute to the manufacture of material goods, and are therefore part of the *industrial* process.

F (page 650)

6. The fastest-growing communication tool ever developed was Alexander Graham Bell's invention, the telephone.

T (page 654)   7. The biggest transnational corporations have greater total sales than the entire economic production of most countries in the world.

F (page 660)   8. Movies like *Titanic* may do well in the United States and United Kingdom, but attract little attention in most other parts of the world, where traditional values regarding personal relationships and marriage are growing stronger.

T (page 661)   9. The 1986 outbreak of BSE (mad cow disease) in British cattle was linked to the practice of feeding traces of animal parts to cattle.

F (page 668)   10. The World Trade Organization (WTO) is made up of representatives elected by the citizens of its member countries.

Essay Questions

1. What are the major influences on social change throughout history? Focus specifically on factors in the physical environment, political organizations, and culture. How did Marx and Weber view each of those factors?

2. What specific factors have influenced social change in the modern period? How have these changes affected the way we live today?

3. Outline Daniel Bell's concept of postindustrial society. Discuss three empirical factors that are *not* taken into account by this concept.

4. Discuss the major factors propelling the process of globalization. Focus particularly on telecommunication, information technology, and the integration of the world economy.

5. How did the political changes following the collapse of the Soviet system affect the process of globalization? Does increasing access to information about people and events around the world affect this process? How was the growth of transnational corporations connected?

6. The text argues that globalization entails a shift in people's "outlook" to a more global perspective. Trace this argument through the notion that it has an effect on people's cultural and personal identity, which they must now actively construct. Have you experienced such effects? Explain.

7. Outline the three perspectives in the globalization debate. Which position do you find most compelling? Why?

8. Discuss the cultural effects of globalization. Do you think these are more a matter of "cultural imperialism" or "fragmentation of cultural forms"? Justify your position.

9. Do you agree with Ulrich Beck, that globalization brings about a "risk society"? Summarize the kinds of risks that are being "manufactured." What specific risks are you most concerned about? Why?

10. What are the goals of the global justice movement? Why has it focused its criticism on organizations like the WTO? Do you agree with the text, that globalization creates a need for new forms of global governance? Do current organizations meet that need? Explain.